Type 2 Diabetes *Cookbook* for Beginners

Naturally Maintain Blood Sugar and Bring Your A1c below 5.7%

Simple, Delicious, Recipes to Take Back Your Wellbeing

Kathleen Rachel Wright

© **Copyright 2023 by Kathleen Rachel Wright- All rights reserved.**

The content contained within this book may not be reproduced, duplicated or transmitted without direct written permission from the author or the publisher.

Under no circumstances will any blame or legal responsibility be held against the publisher, or author, for any damages, reparation, or monetary loss due to the information contained within this book. Either directly or indirectly.

Legal Notice:

This book is copyright protected. This book is only for personal use. You cannot amend, distribute, sell, use, quote or paraphrase any part, or the content within this book, without the consent of the author or publisher.

Disclaimer Notice:

Please note the information contained within this document is for educational and entertainment purposes only. All effort has been executed to present accurate, up to date, and reliable, complete information. No warranties of any kind are declared or implied. Readers acknowledge that the author is not engaging in the rendering of legal, financial, medical or professional advice. The content within this book has been derived from various sources. Please consult a licensed professional before attempting any techniques outlined in this book.

By reading this document, the reader agrees that under no circumstances is the author responsible for any losses, direct or indirect, which are incurred as a result of the use of information contained within this document, including, but not limited to, — errors, omissions, or inaccuracies.

Table of Contents

Introduction 6
An Overwiev of Diabetes 8
   Types of Diabetes 8
   Causes of Diabetes 9
   Difference between type 1 and type 2 Diabetes 10
   How to prevent Diabetes 10
   Get rid of any excess weight. 11
   Increase your physical activity. 11
   Consume a variety of plant-based foods. 11
   Consume a variety of healthful fats. 11
   Avoid trendy diets in favor of healthier alternatives. 11
   How to control sugar level 12

Eating Guidelines for Diabetic Patients 13
   How much should one eat? 14
   What to eat? 15
   What to avoid eating? 16

Breakfast 19
   Asparagus with Egg 20
   Braunschweiger Omelet 20
   Backward Pizza 21
   California Omelet 21
   Buffalo Wing Omelet 22
   Club Omelet 22
   Coconut Flax Bread 23
   Confetti Frittata 23
   Fried Mush 24
   Greek Cheese, Spinach, and Olive Omelet 24
   Parmesan-Rosemary Eggs 24
   Insta-Quiche 25
   Salted Caramel–Cinnamon Pancakes 25
   Monterey Scramble 26
   Unpotato Tortilla 26
   Perfect Protein Pancakes 27
   Pork Rind Waffles 27
   Rosemary Cheese Crackers 28
   Quork 28
   Smoked Salmon and Goat Cheese scramble 29
   Rodeo Eggs 29
   Monterey Jack and Avocado Omelet 29

Vegetarian 30
   Mains Recipes 30
   Asparagus with Curried Walnut Butter 31
   Asparagus with Soy and Sesame Mayonnaise 31
   Cumin Mushrooms 32
   Dragon's Teeth 32
   Japanese Fried Rice 33
   Lemon-Herb Zucchini 33
   Mushroom Risotto 34
   Mushrooms with Bacon, Sun-Dried Tomatoes, and Cheese 34
   Pepperoncini Spinach 35
   Sautéed Mushrooms and Spinach with Pepperoni 35
   Sweet-and-Sour Cabbage 36
   Two-Cheese Cauliflower 36

Grains, Beans, and Legumes Recipes 37
   Avocado and Brown Rice Salad 38
   Balsamic Green Beans with Bacon and Pine Nuts 38
   Black Bean Soup 39
   Frijoles Charros 39
   Garbanzo Stir Fry 40
   Three-grain salad 40
   Braised Green Beans with Pork 40
   Goulash 41
   Hazelnut Green Beans 41
   Hummus 42
   Kale White Bean Pork Soup 42
   Minestrone 43
   Sautéed Sesame Spinach 43

Beef, Pork, and Lamb Recipes 44
   Banh mi Burgers 45
   Beef and Bacon Rice with Pine Nuts 45
   Beef Stroganoff 46
   Bleu Burger 46
   Tokyo Ginger Pork Chops 46
   Bourbon-Maple Glazed Pork Chops 47
   Burger Scramble Florentine 47
   Cauli-Bacon Dish 48
   Easy Italian Beef 48
   Jakarta Steak 49

Joe (Beef) 49
Kalua Pig with Cabbage 50
Lamb Steaks with Lemon, Olives, and Capers 50
Lamb, Feta, and Spinach Burgers 51
Maple-Chipotle Glazed Pork Steaks 51
Maple-Spice Country-Style Ribs 52
Meatza 52
Mediterranean Lamb Burgers 53
Pan-Broiled Steak 53
Mustard-Grilled Pork with Balsamic Onions 54
Mustard-Maple Glazed Pork Steak 54
Middle Eastern Marinated Lamb Kabobs 55
Pepperoncini Beef 55
Poor Man's Poivrade 56
Pork Loin with Red Wine and Walnuts 56
Pork with a Camembert Sauce 57
Rib-Eye Steak with Wine Sauce 57
Roman Lamb Steak 58
Sirloin with Anaheim-Lime Marinade 58
Smothered Burgers 58
Slow-Cooker Pork Chili 59
Zucchini Meat Loaf Italiano 59
Spareribs Adobado 60
Steak au Poivre with Brandy Cream 60

Poultry Recipes 61
Balsamic-Glazed Chicken and Peppers 62
Chicken-Almond Rice 62
Chicken Breasts Stuffed with Artichokes and Garlic Cheese 63
Chicken Burgers with Basil and Sun-Dried Tomatoes 63
Chicken in Creamy Horseradish Sauce 64
Chicken in Creamy Orange Sauce 64
Chicken Skewers Diavolo 65
Cranberry-Peach Turkey Roast 65
Creamy Chicken and Noodles in a Bowl 66
Golden Triangle Chicken Kabobs 66
Lemon-Herb Chicken Breast 67
Skillet Citrus Chicken 67
Super-Easy Turkey Divan 68
Tandoori Chicken 68
Tasty Roasted Chicken 69
Thanksgiving Weekend Curry 69
Turkey with Mushroom Sauce 70

Yucatán Chicken 70

Fish and seafood Recipes 71
Baked Clams 72
Chili-Bacon Scallops 72
Salmon in a Citrus Vinaigrette 73
Gingered Monkfish 73
Glazed Salmon 74
Halibut with Lemon-Herb Sauce 74
Pesto Shrimp 75
Poached Trout with Dill 75
Deviled Pollock 75
Salmon with Pesto Mayonnaise 76
Sizzling Moroccan Shrimp 76
Sun-Dried Tomato-Portobello Salmon Roast 77
Transcendent flounder 77

Soup and Stew Recipes 78
California Soup 79
Sopa Tlalpeño 79
Crab and Asparagus Soup 80
Cream of Mushroom Soup 80
Cream of Salmon Soup 81
Creamy Broccoli Soup 81
Egg Drop Soup 82
Not Pea Soup 82
Old Fashioned Salmon Soup 83
Olive Soup 83
Chinese-Style Tuna Soup 83
Roman Stew 84
Stracciatella 84
Tavern Soup 84

Salad Recipes 85
Asian Ginger Slaw 86
Bacon, Tomato, and Cauliflower Salad 86
Cheddar-Broccoli Salad 87
Chicken Caesar Salad 87
Chicken-Almond Noodle Salad 88
Chicken-Chili-Cheese Salad 88
Chicken-Pecan Salad 89
Classic Spinach Salad 89
Club Sandwich Salad 90
Dilled Chicken Salad 90
Egg Salad 91
Gorgonzola-and-Pesto Caesar Salad 91

Tuna Salad with Lemon and Capers 91
Mixed Greens with Walnuts, Goat Cheese, and Raspberry Dressing 92
Not-Quite-Middle-Eastern Salad 92
Sour Cream and Cuke Salad 92
Sesame-Asparagus Salad 93
Shrimp Caesar Salad 93
Sirloin Salad 94
Unpotato Salad 94
Southwestern Potato Salad 95
Spinach-Plum Salad 95
Toasted Salad 96
Tuna Salad 96

Vegetable and Side Recipes 97
Asparagus with Mushrooms and Hazelnuts 98
Cucumber-Wrapped Vegetable Rolls 98
Cauli-Rice 99
Chard and Cashew Sauté 99
Cauliflower Purée 99
Roasted Asparagus 100
Roasted Cauliflower with Tahini Sauce 100
Roasted Curried Cauliflower 101
Sautéed Collard Greens 101
Stir-Fry Vegetables 102

Sauces, Dipsand Dressing Recipes 103
Aioli 104
Bacon Butter 104
Blue Cheese Steak Butter 104
Cheese Sauce 105
Chili-Cocoa Rub 105
Chipotle Mayonnaise 106
Cinnamon Sugar 106
Cocktail Sauce 106
Classic Rub 107
Coleslaw Dressing 107
Easy Alfredo Sauce 108
French Vinaigrette 108
Italian Vinaigrette 108
Gorgonzola Sauce 109
Maple Butter 109
Maple-Chipotle Glaze 109
Raspberry Vinaigrette 110
Sun-Dried Tomato and Basil Mayonnaise ....
Tangy Honey Mustard Dressing 111
Wasabi Mayonnaise 111

Dessert Recipes 112
Brownies 113
Cheesecake 113
Cinnamon Nuts 114
Cream Cheese Balls 114
Glazed Walnuts 114
Flan 115
Merry Crispness Shortbread 115
Hazelnut Shortbread 116
Lemon-Cheese Mousse 116
Italian Walnut Cake 117
Marbled Cheesecake Muffins 118
Mixed Berry Cups 118
Merry Crispness Shortbread 119
Pumpkin Cheesecake 119

Juice and Smoothies Recipes 120
Apricot-Orange Smoothie 121
Beet Greens Smoothie 121
Broccoli Apple Smoothie 122
Dandelion Smoothie 122
Flax Almond Butter Smoothie 122
Kale Kiwi Smoothie 123
Pineapple Raspberry Smoothie 123
Pomegranate-Blueberry Smoothie 124
Summer Rhubarb Cooler 124
Zucchini Apples Smoothie 125

Meal plan (21 Weeks) 126
Conclusion 128
Measurement conversion chart 137
Cooking Conversion Chart 138

Introduction

If you have diabetes, your body cannot effectively digest and utilize the glucose you consume from your food. There are many different varieties of diabetes, each with its symptoms and causes, but they all have one thing in common: an excessive amount of glucose in the bloodstream. Drugs and/or insulin are used to treat this condition. Preventing certain types of diabetes is possible by leading a healthy lifestyle.

Diabetes Mellitus, also known as type 2 diabetes, is a metabolic condition characterized by abnormally high glucose levels in the bloodstream. Diabetes occurs when sugar is transported from the bloodstream into your cells, where it can be retained or used for energy generation. Insulin is a hormone that is produced by the pancreas. People with diabetes have a condition in which their bodies do not create enough insulin or cannot adequately utilize the insulin they produce.

If you don't manage your diabetes-related increased blood sugar, it might cause damage to your nerves, kidneys, eyes, and other organs.

A spike in blood sugar levels causes the symptoms of diabetes to manifest themselves.

In addition, diabetes manifests itself in the form of increased appetite and thirst, weight loss, frequent urination, decreased vision, extreme weariness, and sores that do not heal.

Diabetes risk can be influenced by various factors, including your environment, family, and pre-existing medical conditions.

As a result, diabetes patients must pay attention to what they eat and how much they consume.

Several factors, such as weight increase, can exacerbate the illness, making it even more important for diabetic patients to maintain a healthy lifestyle and manage their weight.

Obese people have a higher risk of developing type 2 diabetes, also known as adult-onset diabetes or insulin resistance. In this condition, the blood glucose level is constantly high. Fat tissue cells in obese people may metabolize more calories than they can consume. By taking too many nutrients, inflammation stimulates a protein called cytokinesis, which is triggered by the stress in these cells. As a result, cytokines block insulin receptor signals, causing cells to become insulin-resistant over time. Insulin urges the cells to utilize glucose for nourishment. Because your cells are immune to insulin, your body will be unable to convert glucose into energy, resulting in a persistently raised blood glucose level. In addition to lowering normal insulin responses, stress frequently causes cell inflammation and may contribute to heart failure. Obesity or overweight increases the risk of type 2 diabetes, which occurs when the body's cells grow immune to insulin's activity despite enough insulin. Extra weight puts a burden on the insides of human cells. When the cells have more nutrients to absorb than they can handle, the cell's membrane sends a warning signal, instructing it to reduce the insulin cell surface receptors.

One of the apparent diabetes symptoms is insulin resistance and consistently increased blood sugar glucose levels. Diabetic patients are more likely than non-diabetic patients to develop severe heart issues such as diabetic cardiomyopathy, coronary artery disease, and heart failure. Because of the development of fatty substances throughout the arteries, the heart has to work extra hard in obese or diabetic persons to move blood across the body.

Weight loss is an essential strategy for those who are obese, especially those who have type 2 diabetes. Moderate and regular weight loss of at least 5-10 percent will boost insulin activity, lower fasting blood glucose levels, and lessen the requirement for some diabetes medications. In addition, you must track your lifestyle to correct diabetes symptoms or, at the very least, lower your risks of developing diabetes.

Dietary balance and health Physical activity Medications Physical activity is just as important as medication, but an air fryer can help you maintain a healthy and balanced diet. You can lose weight by controlling your diet and analyzing your eating and how it affects your body.

In this book, you will find all you need to know about diabetes and also what one should eat and avoid in this condition.

You will also find several easy-to-make recipes that are low in carbohydrates and help you maintain your blood sugar level and insulin in the body to fight diabetes.

An Overview of Diabetes

It's a long-term condition that develops when the pancreas cannot create sufficient Insulin to fulfill the body's needs or when the insulin it makes isn't used correctly by the body. Insulin is the hormone that helps to keep blood sugar levels under control.

Types of Diabetes

There are different types of diabetes:

Type 1 Diabetes

It is commonly known as insulin-dependent diabetes or juvenile diabetes and is caused by an immune system deficit or an autoimmune disease. Your immune system attacks insulin-producing cells in the pancreas, robbing the body of its ability to produce insulin. It's unclear what causes autoimmune disease or how to treat it properly. However, to live with Type 1 diabetes, you must take insulin.

Type 2 Diabetes

Adult-onset diabetes, also known as non-insulin-dependent diabetes, is caused by the body's insufficient insulin utilization. In the vast majority of diabetics, type 2 diabetes is present. The symptoms are often mistaken for those of type 1 diabetes. However, the problem can be recognized after several years of diagnosis, which is considerably less noticeable when symptoms have already occurred. Type 2 diabetes develops when your blood sugar levels rise, and your body grows resistant to insulin. Insulin resistance is the cause of type 2 diabetes. Obesity is the result of this. In addition, in type 2 diabetes, your pancreas fails to utilize insulin appropriately. This complicates removing sugar from the blood and storing it in the cells for energy. Finally, this will increase the demand for insulin therapy.

Gestational Diabetes

Gestational diabetes is defined as hyperglycemia, or blood glucose levels higher than usual but not high enough to be classified as diabetes. Prenatal tests are used to diagnose gestational diabetes rather than indications like high blood sugar, which can develop during pregnancy. Insulin-blocking hormones released by the placenta are the leading cause of this kind of diabetes. Insulin-blocking substances produced by the placenta induce this type of diabetes.

Causes of Diabetes

Causes of Type 1 Diabetes

Type 1 diabetes has no recognized cause. Insulin-producing cells in the pancreas are hypothesized to be targeted and eliminated by the immune system. The immune system generally destroys viruses and infectious bacteria. Insulin levels in the human body are low or non-existent. As a result, sugar accumulates in the blood instead of being delivered to the cells. Although the specific nature of these factors is unknown, type 1 diabetes is assumed to be caused by a blend of hereditary predisposition and environmental influences. In type 1 diabetes, weight is not regarded to be a role. When the body's immune system (i.e., the body's ability to fight illness) targets and kills the insulin-producing beta cells in the pancreas, type 1 diabetes develops. Type 1 diabetes, according to scientists, is influenced by a mixture of hereditary and environmental factors.

Causes of Prediabetes and Type 2 Diabetes

Your cells can become immune to the effects of insulin in prediabetes, just as they might in type 2 diabetes, and the pancreas is incapable of generating enough insulin to restore this resistance. Therefore, sugar accumulates in the bloodstream rather than going to the cells, where it would be needed for fuel. Although inherited and environmental factors are considered to play a role in the emergence of type 2 diabetes, it is unknown why this occurs. Obesity is connected to type 2 diabetes progression, though not everyone with the illness is obese. The most prevalent type of diabetes is brought on by several variables, including eating choices and genetic makeup.

Here are a few factors:

Genes and family history

A family history of diabetes makes it more likely that a mother will develop gestational diabetes, implying that genes play a role. Mutations can also explain why the disease occurs more commonly among Asians, African Americans, American Indians, and Latinas, Hispanic. Any gene can increase your risk of developing type 2 diabetes or type 1 diabetes. In addition, a person's genetic background can make them more obese, leading to type 2 diabetes.

Overweight, physical inactivity, and obesity

You are significantly more likely to develop type 2 diabetes if you are not consistently participating and are obese or overweight. Insulin resistance, common in people with type 2 diabetes, is often caused by excess weight. In which the body's fat deposits play a significant role. Extra belly fat is linked to insulin resistance, type 2 diabetes, heart disease, and blood vessel disease.

Insulin resistance

Insulin resistance, a disorder in which the body, liver, and fat cells do not process insulin well, is a typical complication of type 2 diabetes. As a result, the body requires more insulin to allow glucose to reach cells. Therefore, the pancreas produces more insulin to meet the increased demand. However, with time, the pancreas becomes incapable of making the required insulin, causing a rise in blood glucose levels.

Difference between type 1 and type 2 Diabetes

Type 1 diabetes is an autoimmune disease. In the case of this disease, the immune system damages the cells that secrete insulin, ultimately preventing the body from producing any insulin. Type 1 diabetes usually appears in childhood and can last a lifespan.

Type 2 diabetes is caused by lifestyle and genetic factors like weight and lethargy. Exercise and diet can often reverse or moderate the condition, which usually begins in adulthood. Type 2 diabetes affects 90-95 percent of people diagnosed with the disease.

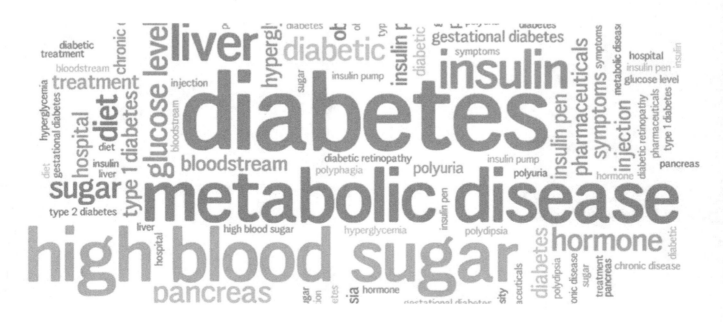

How to prevent Diabetes

Type 2 diabetes, the more prevalent type of the condition, can be prevented by making lifestyle modifications. Prevention is crucial if you have an elevated risk of type 2 diabetes due to excessive weight gain and obesity, high blood cholesterol, or positive family history.

If you have prediabetes, which is high blood sugar but not high enough to be labeled with diabetes, lifestyle adjustments can help you avoid or delay the beginning of the illness.

Making a few lifestyle adjustments now may help you avoid significant diabetes-related health consequences in the future, such as nerve, kidney, and heart damage. It's never too late to start anything new.

Get rid of any excess weight.

There are lower chances of developing diabetes if you lose weight. For example, in one ample research, people reduced their risk of acquiring diabetes by nearly 60% after decreasing around 7% of their body weight with exercise and dietary changes.

Set a weight-loss goal that is proportional to your current body weight. Talk to your doctor about setting realistic short-term goals, such as reducing 1 to 2 pounds weekly.

Increase your physical activity.

Regular physical activity has numerous advantages. Exercise can assist you in the following ways:

Reduce your weight,

Lower your blood sugar and increase your insulin sensitivity, which helps keep your blood sugar in a healthy range.

Consume a variety of plant-based foods.

Vitamins, minerals, and carbohydrates are all found in plants. Carbohydrates contain sugars and starches, which provide energy to the body and fiber. However, dietary fiber is the indigestible portion of plant foods that your body cannot absorb or digest.

Fiber-rich meals help you lose weight and reduce your risk of diabetes. Consume a wide range of nutritious, fiber-rich meals.

Fiber has several advantages, including slowing sugar absorption and reducing blood sugar levels.

Consume a variety of healthful fats.

Foods heavy in fat provide many calories and should be consumed in proportion. Your diet should include a range of foods high in unsaturated fats, sometimes known as "healthy fats," to aid weight loss and management.

Polyunsaturated and monounsaturated fats both promote healthy blood cholesterol levels.

Saturated fats, also known as "bad fats," are found in dairy and animal products. However, these should only make up a small portion of your diet. Low-fat dairy products, as well as lean poultry and pigs, are good sources of saturated fats.

Avoid trendy diets in favor of healthier alternatives.

Many fad diets can help you lose weight, including the glycemic index, paleo, and keto diets. However, there is little evidence of the long-term advantages of these diets or their effectiveness in preventing diabetes.

How to control sugar level

Diabetes management is finding a balance between your medications (insulin or tablets), the foods you eat, and the quantity of exercise you get. A problem with anybody might cause blood sugar levels to spike or plummet. In general, several factors lead to abnormal blood glucose levels. We list some of them below, without claiming to cover them all:

- Failure to take diabetes medication on time
- Failure to stick to the diet plan (e.g., eating too much or too little food without considering the recommendations)
- Failure to exercise regularly
- Excessive stress
- Inability to control blood glucose levels

Monitor your blood sugar levels regularly and track when they are too high or too low. In this way, your diabetic team can make any needed adjustments to your diabetes treatment plan more efficiently.

It's not always easy to keep blood sugars near normal, and no one's blood sugar control is flawless. Even if you do everything you can to stabilize your blood sugar levels, they might sometimes go too high or too low.

- However, there are a few things you can do to help keep your blood sugar levels in a safe range:
- When it comes to insulin or tablets, stick to the schedule.
- As much as feasible, stick to your dietary plan.
- Get some exercise regularly.
- Multiple times a day, monitor your blood sugar level.
- You should see your doctor regularly.
- Learn everything you can about diabetes.

If you follow these instructions, you'll do everything you can to maintain your disease under control.

Here Is How Your Blood Glucose Level Should Look Like

Mg/DL	Fasting	After Eating	2-3 hours After Eating
Normal	80-100	170-200	120-140
Impaired Glucose	101-125	190-230	140-160
Diabetic	126 +	220-300	200 +

Eating Guidelines for Diabetic Patients

Nutritional goals for type 2 Diabetes

Manage your weight

To give yourself the best chance of controlling Type 2 diabetes and avoiding some of the many health risks it can expose you to, you must be at a healthy weight. People who are overweight can improve their diabetes control, lower their blood pressure, and reduce levels of fats in the blood, including cholesterol, by losing weight. A healthy diet and regular exercise are the two critical factors in weight control. This book will help you adapt to a more nutritious diet and also allows you to monitor your calorie intake, so you can see how much energy you need to be using up through exercise.

Balance the blood glucose level

Keeping blood glucose levels within a healthy range is vital in managing diabetes. Too much glucose in the blood for long periods can damage the vessels that supply blood to vital organs such as the heart, kidneys, eyes, and nerves. The type and amount of carbohydrates you eat are the main dietary factors determining blood glucose levels. Slow-release carbohydrates keep blood glucose on an even keel; digested carbohydrates rapidly cause unwelcome surges in blood glucose levels.

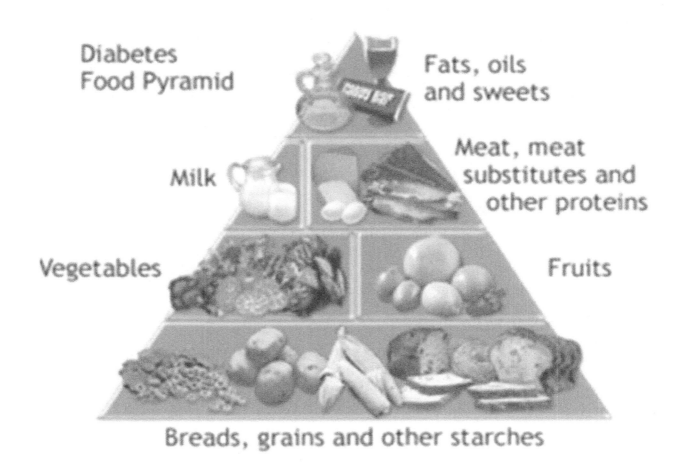

Take care of your heart

People with diabetes are five times more likely to suffer from heart disease or a stroke, so it is vital to eat the right foods to keep your heart healthy. One of the most important steps you can take is to reduce your intake of saturated fat. Saturated fat causes the body to produce cholesterol. In the same way that hard water can clog water pipes and appliances with limescale, cholesterol clogs the blood vessels and causes them to narrow, restricting blood flow to the heart and brain.

Control Blood pressure

High blood pressure increases the risk of heart disease, stroke, and kidney problems. A diet high in sodium is a significant factor in developing high blood pressure, but sodium isn't the whole story. The DASH study (Dietary Approaches to Stop Hypertension) carried out in America found that people who had a moderate sodium intake but who increased their intake of potassium, calcium, and magnesium by eating plenty of fruit, vegetables, and low-fat dairy products, showed more significant reductions in blood pressure that those who restricted sodium. So ask your doctor to check your blood pressure regularly.

Eat more fruits and vegetables

Fruit and vegetables are the cornerstones of a healthy diabetes eating plan. They provide vitamins, minerals, and phytochemicals which, among other benefits, will help to keep your heart and eyes healthy; potassium, which helps to lower blood pressure; and dietary fiber, which encourages the digestive system to function smoothly.

Choose the right carbohydrates

Carbohydrates are converted into glucose, which causes the level of blood glucose to rise. The status to which it grows and the length of time it remains high depend on the type and amount of carbohydrates you eat. Certain carbohydrates are digested more slowly than others, keeping blood glucose levels even and sustaining energy levels. Understanding the effect of carbohydrates on blood glucose levels is the key to living with diabetes

Swap bad fats for good

Reduce your intake of "bad fats"— saturated and trans fats—which increase the risk of heart disease and stroke. Instead, eat more "good fats," such as unsaturated oils, which have a protective effect.

Replace salt with good flavorings

A diet high in sodium is believed to be a significant factor in developing high blood pressure, which represents an increased risk for people with diabetes. On the other hand, experts suggest that reducing sodium intake to no more than 2.4g a day can reduce the risk of stroke or heart attack by a quarter. Instead of relying on salt to make food tasty, use other ways to add flavor.

Lower the sugar intake

Sugar provides what nutritionists call "empty calories"— calories that provide nothing in the way of protein, fiber, vitamins, or minerals and offer no health benefit. Eating large amounts of sugar will cause your blood glucose levels to rise and, in the longer term, can lead to weight gain. You do not need to avoid sugar altogether, but cut back on it as much as possible and try other ways to sweeten food.

How much should one eat?

Your nutritional objective should be to reduce weight and then keep that weight off in the future. Healthy eating habits must consequently involve a method you can stick to for the rest of your life. Making healthy choices that match some of your cuisines and traditional preferences might be beneficial.

Divide your plate as a simple method to help you make excellent meal choices and consume proper portion sizes.

These three divisions on your plate encourage you to eat healthily:

- Half of your plate should include fruit and non-starchy veggies.
- Whole grains account for one-quarter of the diet.
- Protein-rich foods, such as beans, seafood, and lean meats, account for one-quarter of the diet.

What to eat?

If you have type 2 diabetes, choose a diet high in nutrient-dense foods to help your body get the fiber, vitamins, and minerals it requires.

Monounsaturated and polyunsaturated fatty acids and other heart-healthy fats should be included in your diet.

Similarly, consuming various high-fiber foods might help manage blood sugar levels and keep you feeling fuller for longer, preventing you from eating when you aren't hungry.

In addition, your diet should be easy to follow and maintain. Diets that are too restrictive or do not fit your lifestyle can be challenging to maintain over time.

Here are some foods that should be included in your diet:
- Vegetables (broccoli, cauliflower, spinach, cucumbers, zucchini)
- Legumes (beans, lentils, chickpeas)
- Seeds (chia seeds, pumpkin seeds
- Fruits (apples, oranges, berries, melons, pears, peaches)
- Whole grains (quinoa, couscous, oats, brown rice, emmer)
- Nuts (almonds, walnuts, pistachios, macadamia nuts, cashews)
- Fla (water, black coffee, unsweetened tea, vegetable juice).

What to avoid eating?

Beverages with added sugar

Sweetened beverages are the worst drinks for people with diabetes to consume.

They're rich in carbs, with 38.5 g in a 12-ounce (354-mL) can of cola.

Sugary lemonade and iced tea include nearly 45 g of sugar-only carbohydrates.

Furthermore, these beverages are high in fructose, which is related to diabetes and insulin resistance. According to research, consuming sugar-sweetened beverages has increased risk of diabetes-related illnesses such as fatty liver disease.

Furthermore, sweetened drinks' high fructose content may cause metabolic alterations that encourage belly fat and possibly hazardous triglyceride and cholesterol levels.

Rather than sweetened beverages, drink club soda, water, or unsweetened iced tea to help manage blood sugar levels and reduce illness risk.

Trans fats

Trans fats that have been synthesized are exceedingly harmful.

They're made by making unsaturated fatty acids more persistent by adding hydrogen.

Margarine, peanut butter, spreads, frozen dinners, and creamers include trans fats. Furthermore, they are frequently added to crackers, muffins, and other baked items to help increase the product's shelf life.

Trans fats have been associated with increased insulin resistance, inflammation, and abdominal fat, as well as decreased levels of good cholesterol and reduced vascular function, despite not directly affecting blood sugar levels.

Any product with the phrase "partially hydrogenated" in the ingredient list should be avoided.

Pasta, white bread, and rice

Processed foods like rice, white bread, and pasta are high in carbs.

In persons with type 1 and type 2 diabetes, eating bagels, bread, and other refined-flour items has been shown to raise blood sugar levels drastically.

This reaction isn't limited to refined white flour-based items. For example, in one study, gluten-free pasta was also found to elevate blood sugar levels, with rice-based varieties having the most significant effect.

In another study, high-carbohydrate diets increased blood sugar levels and reduced brain function in persons with mental impairments and type 2 diabetes.

Fiber is scarce in these processed foods. Fiber aids in the slowing of sugar absorption into the bloodstream.

Increased fiber consumption increases gut microbiota, which may result in a reduction in insulin resistance.

Yogurt with fruit flavors

Plain yogurt might be a healthy choice for people with diabetes. Fruit-flavored versions, on the other hand, are a different story.

Flavored yogurts are usually manufactured with low-fat or nonfat milk and are high in sugar and carbohydrates.

Frozen yogurt is widely regarded as a healthy option for ice cream. It can, however, hold just as much, if not more, sugar as ice cream.

Rather than picking high-sugar yogurts and risk having insulin and blood sugar spikes, go for plain, whole milk yogurt, which has no added sugar and may help with hunger management, losing weight, and gastrointestinal health.

Breakfast cereals with added sugar

If you have diabetes, cereal is among the deadliest ways to begin your day.

Despite health recommendations on their labels, most cereals are heavily processed and include significantly more carbohydrates than many consumers realize.

Furthermore, they contain a meager protein that can assist you in feeling fuller throughout the day while consistently maintaining your blood sugar levels.

Even certain "healthy" breakfast cereals are not recommended for people with diabetes.

Skip most cereals in favor of a protein-based, low-carb breakfast to control appetite and blood sugar.

Coffee drinks with different flavors

Coffee has been connected to various health advantages and a lower incidence of diabetes.

Flavored coffee drinks, on the other hand, should be considered a liquid treat instead of a wholesome beverage.

According to studies, your brain does not handle solid and liquid foods similarly. As a result, when you consume calories, you don't make up for it later by eating less, which might lead to weight gain.

Carbohydrates abound in flavored coffee drinks.

Choose espresso or regular coffee with a spoonful of half-and-half or heavy cream to maintain your blood sugar in check and prevent weight gain.

Honey, maple syrup, and agave nectar

People with diabetes generally avoid white sugar and delicacies like cookies, candy, and pie.

On the other hand, other types of sugar can produce blood sugar rises. Brown sugar and "natural" sugars like honey, maple syrup, and agave nectar are examples.

Even though these sweeteners aren't heavily processed, they have about the same carbohydrates as white sugar. However, the majority of them have much more.

Avoiding all types of sugar and replacing it with natural low-carb sweeteners is the best method.

Fruit that has been dried

Fruit is high in potassium, vitamin C, and other vital minerals and vitamins.

Fruit is dried, which causes a lack of moisture, resulting in even larger quantities of essential nutrients.

Regrettably, the amount of sugar in it increases as well.

Raisins have more than four times the amount of carbohydrates as grapes. The Carbohydrate Content of other varieties of dried fruit is similar to that of fresh fruit.

You don't have to surrender fruit entirely if you have diabetes. Adhering to low-sugar foods like a small apple or fresh berries will help you maintain a healthy blood sugar level while staying within the goal range.

Snacks in packages

Snacks such as crackers, pretzels, and other packaged foods are not recommended.

They're usually produced with refined flour and contain few nutrients, but they're high in fast-digesting carbohydrates that spike blood sugar quickly.

According to one study, snack foods include 7.7% more carbohydrates on average than the labeled claims.

If you're hungry between meals, almonds or a few low-carb vegetables with some cheese are a better option.

Juice from fruits

Although fruit juice is frequently seen as a healthful beverage, its blood sugar effects are identical to other sugary drinks and sodas. This applies to unsweetened 100 percent fruit juice and juice with added sugar. In addition, in some circumstances, fruit juice has a higher carbohydrate and sugar content than soda.

Fruit juice, like sugar-sweetened beverages, is high in fructose. Obesity, insulin resistance, and heart disease are all caused by fructose.

Water with a slice of lemon is a far better option, as it contains less than a gram of carbohydrate and is almost calorie-free.

French Fries

One of the foods you should avoid if you have diabetes is French fries.

Carbohydrate content in potatoes is relatively high.

Potatoes may do more than raise your blood sugar once fried.

Frequent consumption of french fries and other fried meals has been related to cancer and heart disease in various studies.

If you don't want to eliminate potatoes, a modest dish of sweet potatoes is the ideal alternative.

Breakfast

Asparagus with Egg

 Prep Time: 10 minutes Cook Time: 15 minutes Servings: 4

Directions

1. Preheat the oven to broil.
2. Break the asparagus tips off where they typically break. Place the asparagus spears in a microwave-safe baking dish or a glass pie plate. Cover with a couple of teaspoons of water.
3. Microwave for four minutes on high.
4. Mash the garlic cloves into the olive oil while the asparagus is cooking.
5. Drain the asparagus when it's done.
6. Asparagus should be divided among the four dishes. If not, a rectangle glass baking dish will be required.
7. In the baking dish, arrange the asparagus in four groups.
8. Drizzle garlic oil over each serving of asparagus.
9. Season with a pinch of salt and pepper, then divide the cheese among the four plates. Place the asparagus underneath the broiler at a distance of 4 inches (10 cm) from the heat source.
10. Allow for five minutes of broiling.
11. Fry the eggs to your taste while the asparagus is broiling. To cook them all at once, use your largest pan, or divide them between two skillets.
12. Remove the asparagus from the grill when the Parmesan is faintly browned.
13. Remove the asparagus from the grill when the Parmesan is faintly browned.
14. Carefully transfer each serving to a plate with a large spatula.
15. Serve two fried eggs on top of each asparagus portion.

Nutrition: 310 Calories| Fat: 25g| Protein: 16g| Carbohydrates: 4g

Ingredients

- One pound of asparagus
- One clove of garlic, crushed
- A quarter cup of olive oil
- Salt and ground black pepper to taste
- Half cup of grated Parmesan cheese
- Eight eggs

Braunschweiger Omelet

Ingredients

- One tablespoon of butter
- Two eggs, beaten
- Two ounces of braunschweiger (liverwurst), mashed a bit with a fork
- A quarter medium ripe tomato, sliced
- Mayonnaise (optional)

 Prep Time: 10 minutes Cook Time: 8 minutes Servings: 1

Directions

1. Make your omelet, spoon the mashed braunschweiger over half of your omelet, and top with the tomato slices. If you'd like to gild the lily, a dollop of mayonnaise is good on top of this.

Nutrition: 443 Calories| Fat: 39g|Protein: 19g|Carbohydrates: 4g

Backward Pizza

Prep Time: 10 minutes **Cook Time:** 20 minutes **Servings:** 6

Ingredients

- One clove of garlic
- Three tablespoons of olive oil
- 1/3 cup of no-sugar-added pizza sauce
- One and a half teaspoons of dried oregano
- Half cup of mozzarella cheese, grated
- Half teaspoon of red pepper flakes (optional)
- A quarter cup of grated Parmesan cheese

Directions

1. Preheat the oven to 375°F.
2. Line a jelly roll tin with non-stick foil.
3. Spread the mozzarella evenly over the foil, all the way to the corners.
4. Bake for 5 minutes, turn the pan to help it cook evenly, and give it another 5 to 7 minutes—you want the cheese golden brown all over.
5. While the cheese is baking, crush the garlic into a little cup and cover with the olive oil, stirring once.
6. Put your pizza sauce in a microwavable dish and give it 1 minute to warm.
7. When your cheese is an even, golden layer, pull it out of the oven. Drizzle the garlicky oil all over it, spreading with a brush or the back of a spoon.
8. Sprinkle with oregano and red pepper flakes if using.
9. Spread the pizza sauce over the oil and sprinkle the Parmesan over that. Cut into six big rectangles to serve.

Nutrition: 262 Calories| Fat: 22g| Protein: 14g| Carbohydrates: 3g

California Omelet

Prep Time: 5 minutes **Cook Time:** 5 minutes **Servings:** 1

Ingredients

- One tablespoon of olive oil
- Two eggs, beaten
- Two ounces of Monterey Jack cheese, shredded
- A quarter avocado, sliced
- A quarter cup of alfalfa sprouts

Directions

1. When ready to add the filling, place the Monterey Jack over half of your omelet.
2. Cover, turn the heat to low, and cook until the cheese is melted (2 to 3 minutes).
3. Arrange the avocado and sprouts over the cheese and follow the directions to finish making the omelet.

Nutrition: 545 Calories| Fat: 47g| Protein: 26g| Carbohydrates: 5g

Buffalo Wing Omelet

 Prep Time: 5 minutes   **Cook Time:** 5 minutes   **Servings:** 1

Directions

1. Make your omelet using the bacon grease for the fat. Then, fill with the blue cheese.
2. While your omelet is covered on low heat, melt the cheese and butter with the Tabasco sauce in a small saucepan or nuke for a minute in a custard cup.
3. Stir them together well.
4. When your omelet's done, fold and plate, and then top with the sauce and eat.

Nutrition: 384 Calories| Fat:34g| Protein:17g| Carbohydrates:2g

Ingredients

- One and a half teaspoons of bacon grease
- Two eggs, beaten
- Three tablespoons of crumbled blue cheese
- One tablespoon of butter
- One tablespoon of hot sauce (preferably Frank's Red Hot, Tabasco, or Louisiana brand)

Club Omelet

 Prep Time: 10 minutes   **Cook Time:** 8 minutes   **Servings:** 1

Directions

1. Cook and drain your bacon.
2. Cut the turkey into small squares and slice the tomato and scallion.
3. Beat the eggs, and make your omelet, using a couple of spoonfuls of the bacon grease.
4. Add just the bacon and turkey before covering. Once cooked to your liking, sprinkle the tomato and scallion over the meat, spread the mayonnaise on the other side, fold, and serve.

Nutrition: 383 Calories| Fat: 28g| Protein: 29g| Carbohydrates: 5g

Ingredients

- Two slices of bacon
- Two ounces of sliced turkey breast
- Half small tomato
- One scallion
- Two eggs
- One tablespoon of mayonnaise

Coconut Flax Bread

Prep Time: 10 minutes
Cook Time: 1 h 20 min
Servings: 20 slices

Ingredients

- Four cups of shredded coconut meat
- 3/4 cup of flaxseed meal
- One tablespoon of xanthan or guar
- One teaspoon of erythritol
- One and a half teaspoons of baking soda
- Half teaspoon of salt
- Half a cup of water
- Two tablespoons of cider vinegar
- Four eggs

Directions

1. Preheat the oven to 350 degrees Fahrenheit.
2. Grease a typical loaf pan, not a super-large one. Using nonstick aluminum foil or baking paper, line the pan.
3. Combine the flaxseed meal, coconut, xanthan gum, baking soda, erythritol, and salt in a food processor fitted with the S-blade.
4. Run the machine until all of the ingredients are finely ground. Then, scrape down the sides of the processor and run it again.
5. While that's happening, combine the water and vinegar in a glass measuring cup. Place this near the food processor.
6. Add the eggs one at a time through the feed tube while the food processor runs.
7. Finally, through the feed tube, pour in the water-and-vinegar combination. Just another 30 seconds or so of running.
8. Scoop or transfer the batter into the loaf pan that has been prepared. Preheat the oven to 350°F and bake for 1 hour and 15 minutes. Allow cooling on a wire rack.
9. This is an excellent slicer. Refrigerate this or, better yet, slice it and freeze it as soon as it's cool.

Nutrition: 111 Calories| Fat: 9g| Protein: 4g| Carbohydrates: 5g

Confetti Frittata

Prep Time: 10 minutes
Cook Time: 30 minutes
Servings: 4

Ingredients

- Four ounces of bulk pork sausage
- A quarter cup of diced green bell pepper
- A quarter cup of diced red bell pepper
- A quarter cup of diced sweet red onion
- A quarter cup of grated Parmesan cheese
- One teaspoon of original flavor Mrs. Dash
- Eight eggs, beaten

Directions

1. Preheat the oven to broil.
2. Brown and crumble the sausage in a large, ovenproof skillet over medium heat.
3. Add the onions and peppers to the skillet as the fat renders.
4. Sauté the sausage and vegetables until the sausage is no longer pink.
5. In the bottom of the skillet, spread the mixture into an equal layer.
6. Whisk together the eggs, Parmesan cheese, and seasonings in a medium bowl, then pour over the sausage and vegetables in the skillet.
7. Reduce to a low heat setting and cover the skillet. (If your skillet doesn't come with a lid, cover it with foil.)
8. Cook until the eggs are mostly set in the frittata. This could take up to 25 or 30 minutes, but the size of your skillet will influence how quickly it cooks, so keep an eye on it.
9. When the frittata has all set except for the very top, place it under the broiler for about 5 minutes or until the top is brown. Serve wedges cut into wedges.

Nutrition: 279 Calories| Fat: 22g| Protein: 16g| Carbohydrates: 4g

Fried Mush

Ingredients

- Four eggs
- Half cup of ricotta cheese
- A quarter cup of heavy cream
- Thirty-six drops of liquid stevia
- Half teaspoon of ground cinnamon
- A quarter teaspoon of ground nutmeg
- Six drops of corn flavoring (optional)
- One teaspoon of oil

 Prep Time: 10 minutes   Cook Time: 30 minutes   Servings: 4

Directions

1. Preheat the oven to 350°F. Coat an 8-inch (20 cm) square baking dish with non-stick cooking spray.
2. Simply put everything but the oil in a mixing bowl. Whisk together and pour into the prepared baking dish.
3. Bake for 25 minutes until a knife inserted in the center comes out clean. Pull it out of the oven and let it cool for a few minutes.
4. Put your large, heavy skillet over medium heat, and add the oil. Cut the mush into four squares, and fry until they're golden on both sides. Serve with Cinnamon "Sugar."

Nutrition: 232 Calories| Fat: 21g| Protein: 9g| Carbohydrates: 2g

Greek Cheese, Spinach, and Olive Omelet

Ingredients

- One tablespoon of olive oil
- Two eggs, beaten
- Two tablespoons of crumbled feta cheese
- Two tablespoons of shredded kasseri cheese
- Half cup of chopped fresh spinach or baby spinach leaves
- Four kalamata olives, pitted and chopped

 Prep Time: 7 minutes   Cook Time: 6 minutes   Servings: 1

Directions

1. Make your omelet using olive oil for the fat.
2. Layer in the cheeses, then the spinach, with the chopped olives on top. Let it cook until the cheese is hot and the spinach starts to wilt a bit.

Nutrition: 457Calories| Fat: 40g| Protein: 4g| Carbohydrates: 4g

Parmesan-Rosemary Eggs

Ingredients

- Six eggs
- Half cup of grated Parmesan cheese
- A quarter cup of heavy cream
- One teaspoon of ground rosemary
- One clove of garlic, crushed
- One tablespoon of butter

 Prep Time: 10 minutes   Cook Time: 8 minutes   Servings: 2

Directions

1. Whisk together the eggs, cheese, cream, rosemary, and garlic. Put a large skillet over medium-high heat (if it isn't non-stick, give it a shot of non-stick cooking spray first).
2. When the pan is hot, add the butter, give the egg mixture one last stir to make sure the cheese hasn't settled to the bottom, then pour the egg mixture into the skillet.
3. Scramble until the eggs are set and serve.

Nutrition: 448 Calories| Fat: 36g| Protein: 26g| Carbohydrates: 4g

Insta-Quiche

Prep Time: 10 minutes Cook Time: 15 minutes Servings: 4

Ingredients

- Eight slices of bacon
- Five eggs
- A quarter cup of heavy cream
- A quarter cup of carb-reduced milk or sugar-free almond milk
- One tablespoon of dry vermouth
- Half teaspoon of salt
- A quarter teaspoon of ground black pepper
- A pinch of ground nutmeg
- One tablespoon of butter
- Eight ounces of shredded Swiss cheese

Directions

1. Place a 10-inch (25 cm) non-stick skillet over medium heat. Let it heat.
2. Lay the bacon on a microwave bacon rack or in a microwavable baking dish. Stick it in the microwave on high for 8 to 9 minutes. (The length of time will depend a bit on your microwave.)
3. Whisk together the eggs, cream, carb-reduced milk, vermouth, salt, pepper, and nutmeg in a medium mixing bowl.
4. Put your butter in your now-hot skillet and swirl it around as it melts to coat the bottom. Now pour in your egg mixture.
5. Use a spatula—preferably one for non-stick skillets—to gently stir the eggs around, pulling back the part that's setting and letting the liquid egg run underneath. It won't work like an omelet, where it sets up firm enough that you can lift the whole edge.
6. Just scramble them gently until they're about half-set, half-liquid.
7. Spread the eggs evenly in the skillet and sprinkle the shredded cheese over the top. Cover the skillet and turn the burner to low. (If you have an electric stove, you'll need to shift your pan to a low burner.)
8. Turn on the broiler and set the rack 4 inches (10 cm) below it.
9. When the bacon is done, take it out, drain it, and let it cool for just a minute or two. Then crumble it, or easier, you can use your kitchen shears to snip it into bits. Next, uncover your Insta-Quiche and sprinkle the bacon bits evenly over the top.
10. Now slide the whole thing under the broiler for just a minute until you're sure the top is set, then cut into wedges and Serve

Nutrition: 438 Calories| Fat: 34g| Protein: 28g| Carbohydrates: 4g

Salted Caramel–Cinnamon Pancakes

Prep Time: 15 minutes Cook Time: 20 minutes Servings: 3

Ingredients

- Three and a half ounces of plain pork rinds or skins
- One teaspoon of ground cinnamon
- Half teaspoon of baking powder
- Four eggs
- Half cup of heavy cream
- A quarter teaspoon of liquid stevia (English toffee), or more to taste
- Water, as needed
- Three tablespoons of butter, plus more for serving
- Three tablespoons of caramel sugar-free coffee flavoring syrup

Directions

1. Run the pork rinds through your food processor till you have fine crumbs. Dump them in a mixing bowl.
2. Add the cinnamon and baking powder and stir them into the crumbs.
3. In a separate bowl, whisk together the eggs, cream, and stevia. Pour this into the crumbs and whisk till everything's evenly wet.
4. Let this mixture sit for 5 minutes or so. This would be a good time to put your frying pan or griddle over medium heat; you'll want it hot when the batter is ready.
5. Come back to your batter. It will have been thick to start with and will have thickened even more on standing, becoming downright gloppy. Thin it with water to a consistency you like.
6. Melt half of the butter in your skillet or on the griddle and start frying your pancakes like you would any pancakes.
7. Let them get nicely browned on the first side before flipping and cooking the other. The rest of the butter is for the second round, of course.
8. Serve with more butter and a sprinkle of Cinnamon sugar.

Nutrition: 508 Calories| Fat: 42g| Protein: 29g| Carbohydrates: 3g

Monterey Scramble

 Prep Time: 10 minutes   Cook Time: 8 minutes   Servings: 2

Directions

1. Thinly slice your artichoke hearts, slice your scallions, shred your cheese and have them standing by.
2. Scramble up your eggs with the pesto until it is completely blended in.
3. Give your medium skillet a squirt of non-stick cooking spray and put it over medium-high heat. Add the butter and let it melt.
4. Throw your veggies in the skillet and pour the eggs on top. Scramble it all together until the eggs are set almost to your liking.
5. Scatter the cheese over the top, cover the skillet, turn off the burner, and let the residual heat melt the cheese and finish cooking the eggs.

Nutrition: 449 Calories| Fat: 36g| Protein: 26g| Carbohydrates: 5g

Ingredients

- Two canned artichoke hearts
- Two scallions
- One ounce of Monterey Jack cheese
- Three eggs
- One teaspoon of pesto sauce
- One tablespoon of butter

Unpotato Tortilla

 Prep Time: 10 minutes   Cook Time: 20 minutes   Servings: 6

Directions

1. Reduce the heat to low and preheat the broiler.
2. Cauliflower should be thinly sliced, including the stem, and turnips should be peeled and thinly sliced.
3. Put them in a microwave-safe casserole dish with a lid, add a few tablespoons of water, and cook for 6 to 7 minutes on high.
4. Meanwhile, start sautéing the onion in two tablespoons of olive oil in an 8- to 9-inch (20- to 23-cm) pan—a non-stick skillet is preferred, but not required—in an 8- to 9-inch (20- to 23-cm) skillet. Give your skillet a nice squirt of non-stick cooking spray if it isn't already non-stick.
5. Use a medium heat setting.
6. Pull the vegetables out of the microwave when it beeps, drain them, and toss them in the skillet with the onion. Continue to sauté everything, adding a little extra oil if things start to stick, for approximately 10 to 15 minutes, or until the veggies are golden around the edges.
7. Reduce the heat to low and arrange the vegetables in an equal layer on the skillet's bottom.
8. Combine the eggs, salt, and pepper in a mixing bowl, and pour over the vegetables. Cook for 5–7 minutes on low, raising the edges regularly to allow raw egg to run underneath.
9. When everything is ready except the top, place the skillet under a low broiler for 4 to 5 minutes or until the tortilla is brown on top. (Wrap your skillet in foil first if it doesn't have a flameproof handle.) To serve, cut into wedges. It's good to include a little minced parsley on top, but it's not required.

Nutrition: 139 Calories| Fat: 11g| Protein: 6g| Carbohydrates: 1g

Ingredients

- A quarter head cauliflower
- One medium turnip
- One medium onion, sliced thin
- Three tablespoons of olive oil, divided
- Six eggs
- Salt and ground black pepper to taste
- Chopped fresh parsley (optional)

Perfect Protein Pancakes

 Prep Time: 10 minutes Cook Time: 8 minutes Servings: 30 pancakes

Directions

1. Coat a heavy skillet or griddle with non-stick cooking spray and place it over medium heat.
2. Whisk the eggs and ricotta together in a mixing bowl until quite smooth. Next, whisk in the protein powder, baking powder, and salt, only mixing until well combined.
3. Melt one tablespoon of the butter on the hot skillet or griddle and drop the batter onto it by the tablespoonful.
4. When the bubbles on the surface of the pancakes break and leave little holes around the edges, flip them and cook the other side.
5. Add the rest of the butter to cook the rest of the batter.
6. Serve these with Maple Butter or Cinnamon "Sugar."

Nutrition: 45 Calories| Fat: 3g| Protein: 5g| Carbohydrates: 1g

Ingredients

- Four eggs
- One cup of ricotta cheese
- Half cup of vanilla whey protein powder
- One teaspoon of baking powder
- A quarter teaspoon of salt
- Two tablespoons of butter

Pork Rind Waffles

 Prep Time: 15 minutes Cook Time: 20 minutes Servings: 12 waffles

Directions

1. Plug in your waffle iron. You want it hot when the batter is ready.
2. Run the pork rinds through your food processor until they're powdered. Dump the pork rind crumbs into a mixing bowl.
3. Add the erythritol, protein powder, almond meal, baking powder, and cinnamon. Use a whisk to stir everything together well.
4. Separate the eggs, put the whites into a deep, narrow mixing bowl, and put the yolks in with the pork rind mixture.
5. Since the tiniest speck of yolk will keep your egg whites from whipping, do yourself a favor and separate each one into a custard cup first.
6. Whisk the egg yolks and the water into the pork rind mixture. Let this sit while you do the next step.
7. Using an electric mixer, whip the egg whites until they stand in stiff peaks. With a rubber scraper, gently fold the egg whites into the pork rind mixture, adding one-quarter of the whites and incorporating them well before adding another quarter, and so on.
8. Bake the batter according to the instructions that come with your waffle iron.
9. Serve immediately, with butter and Cinnamon "Sugar" or Maple Butter.
10. To freeze, cool on paper towels to absorb moisture, then put in resealable plastic bags with the towels still between them.
11. Reheat in the toaster or toaster oven rather than the microwave, so your waffles will be crisp.

Ingredients

- Three and a half ounces of plain pork rinds or skins
- A quarter cup of erythritol
- A quarter cup of vanilla whey protein powder
- A quarter cup of almond meal
- Half teaspoon of baking powder
- A quarter teaspoon of ground cinnamon
- Five eggs
- One and a half cups of water

Nutrition: 103 Calories| Fat: 5g| Protein: 12g| Carbohydrates: 2g

Rosemary Cheese Crackers

Prep Time: 10 minutes
Cook Time: 25 minutes
Servings: 50 crackers

Ingredients

- One cup of sunflower seed kernels
- Half cup of rice protein powder
- Half a teaspoon of xanthan or guar
- Half teaspoon of baking powder
- Half teaspoon of salt, plus more for sprinkling
- Two tablespoons of butter at room temperature
- One and a half tablespoons of minced fresh rosemary
- One cup of shredded sharp Cheddar cheese
- Half cup of shredded Parmesan cheese
- One egg white
- Three tablespoons of water

Directions

1. Preheat the oven to 350°F.
2. Put the sunflower seeds, rice protein powder, xanthan or guar, baking powder, and salt in your food processor, and run till the sunflower seeds are ground up to the texture of cornmeal or finer.
3. With the processor running, add the butter and the rosemary. Then work in the cheeses in 3 or 4 additions.
4. With the processor still running, add the egg white, then the water. When you have a soft dough, turn off the processor.
5. Line a cookie sheet with baking parchment. Make a ball of half the dough, and put it on the parchment, then put another sheet of parchment over it.
6. Use your rolling pin to roll the dough out into as thin and even a sheet as you can. Carefully peel off the top sheet of parchment.
7. Use a straight, thin-bladed knife to score the dough into crackers. Sprinkle them lightly with salt.
8. Bake for 20 to 25 minutes or until golden. Score again before removing it from the parchment.

Nutrition: 42 Calories| Fat: 3g| Protein: 3g| Carbohydrates: 1g

Quork

Prep Time: 10 minutes
Cook Time: 55 minutes
Servings: 8

Ingredients

- Seven ounces of plain pork rinds or skins
- Half cup of butter
- Half teaspoon of liquid stevia (English toffee)
- A quarter teaspoon of corn flavoring (optional)
- One cup of erythritol

Directions

1. Preheat the oven to 275°F (130°C). While it's heating, break your pork rinds up into bits about the size of cold cereal.
2. When the oven is hot, put the butter in your biggest roasting pan and put it in the oven to melt.
3. When the butter is melted, pull the pan out of the oven. Add the liquid stevia, and corn flavoring is used. Stir them into the butter.
4. Add the pork rinds to the pan, and, using a pancake turner, stir them into the butter until they're all evenly coated.
5. Sprinkle the erythritol over the pork rinds a quarter cup at a time, stirring each addition well before adding more.
6. When all the erythritol is worked in, slide the pan back into the oven. Toast the pork rinds for 40 minutes, stirring everything very well with a pancake-turner every 10 minutes.
7. At the end of 40 minutes, remove from the oven and let your Quork cool in the pan before storing it in an airtight container.

Nutrition: 237 Calories| Fat: 19g| Protein: 15g| Carbohydrates: 0g

Smoked Salmon and Goat Cheese scramble

Ingredients
- Four eggs
- Half cup of heavy cream
- One teaspoon of dried dill weed
- Four scallions
- Four ounces of chèvre (goat cheese)
- Four ounces of moist smoked salmon
- Two tablespoons of butter

 Prep Time: 10 minutes  Cook Time: 8 minutes Servings: 3

Directions
1. Combine the eggs, cream, and dill in a mixing bowl. Thinly slice the scallions, including the crisp green part.
2. Cut the chèvre into little hunks with a texture comparable to cream cheese. Shred the smoked salmon coarsely.
3. Melt the butter in a large (ideally nonstick) skillet over medium-high heat. (If your skillet's surface isn't nonstick, spray it with nonstick cooking spray before adding the butter.)
4. When the butter has melted, toss in the scallions and cook for a minute.
5. Add the egg mixture and cook, constantly stirring, for 60 to 90 seconds, or until the eggs are halfway set. Add the smoked salmon and chèvre, and heat, constantly stirring, until the eggs are set.

Nutrition: 407 Calories| Fat: 31g| Protein: 27g| Carbohydrates: 5g

Rodeo Eggs

Ingredients
- Four slices of bacon, chopped into 1-inch pieces
- Four thin slices of onion—round slices through the equator
- Four eggs
- Four thin slices of Cheddar cheese

 Prep Time: 10 minutes  Cook Time: 15 minutes Servings: 1

Directions
1. Begin frying the bacon in a heavy skillet over medium heat. When some fat has cooked out of it, push it aside and put the onion slices in, too.
2. Fry the onion on each side, turning carefully to keep the slices together until it starts to look translucent. Remove the onion from the skillet and set it aside.
3. Continue frying the bacon until it's crisp. Pour off most of the grease and distribute the bacon bits evenly over the bottom of the skillet.
4. Break in the eggs and fry for a minute or two until the bottoms are set, but the tops are still soft. (If you like your yolks hard, break them with a fork; if you like them soft, leave them unbroken.)
5. Place a slice of onion over each yolk, then cover the onion with a slice of cheese. Add a teaspoon of water to the skillet, cover, and cook for 2 to 3 minutes, or until the cheese is thoroughly melted.
6. Cut into four separate pieces with the edge of a spatula and serve.

Nutrition: 438 Calories| Fat: 34g| Protein: 29g| Carbohydrates: 3g

Monterey Jack and Avocado Omelet

Ingredients
- Two eggs, beaten
- Two teaspoons of butter
- One ounce of Monterey Jack, pepper Jack, or Cheddar cheese, sliced or shredded
- Half avocado, sliced

 Prep Time: 2 minutes  Cook Time: 5 minutes Servings: 1

Directions
1. Just make a regular omelet.
2. Add the cheese, turn the burner to low, cover, and let the cheese melt. Finally, add the avocado just before folding.

Nutrition: 372 Calories| Fat: 32g| Protein: 19g| Carbohydrates: 7g

Vegetarian Mains Recipes

Asparagus with Curried Walnut Butter

Prep Time: 10 minutes
Cook Time: 16 minutes
Servings: 3

Directions

1. Snap the ends off of the asparagus where they want to break naturally. Put in a microwavable container with a lid or use a glass pie plate and plastic wrap. Either way, add a tablespoon or two (15 to 28 ml) of water and cover.
2. Microwave on high for 5 minutes. Don't forget to uncover it as soon as the microwave goes beep, or your asparagus will keep cooking.
3. While that's cooking, put the butter in a medium skillet over medium heat. When it's melted, add the walnuts. Stir them around for 2 to 3 minutes until they're getting toasty.
4. Now stir in the curry powder, cumin, and stevia, and stir for another 2 minutes or so.
5. Your asparagus is done by now. Fish it out of the container with tongs, put it on your serving plates, and top with the curried walnut butter.

Nutrition: 189 Calories| Fat: 19g| Protein: 3g| Carbohydrates: 5g

Ingredients

- One pound of asparagus
- A quarter cup of butter
- Two tablespoons of chopped walnuts
- One teaspoon of curry powder
- Half teaspoon of ground cumin
- Nine drops of liquid stevia (English toffee)

Asparagus with Soy and Sesame Mayonnaise

Ingredients

- One pound of asparagus
- Half cup of mayonnaise
- Two teaspoons of soy sauce
- One teaspoon of dark sesame oil
- A quarter teaspoon of chili garlic sauce
- One scallion

Prep Time: 10 minutes
Cook Time: 20 minutes
Servings: 3

Directions

1. Snap the ends off the asparagus where they want to break naturally. Put them in a microwave steamer or a glass pie plate.
2. Add a couple of tablespoons (28 ml) of water, cover, and nuke on high for 5 minutes.
3. In the meantime, combine everything else in your food processor with the S-blade in place and run until the scallion is pulverized.
4. The standard way to serve this is to give everyone a puddle of sauce in which to dip their asparagus.
5. The fancy way is to spoon the sauce into a baggie, snip a teeny bit off the corner, and pipe artistic squiggles of sauce over your plates of asparagus.

Nutrition: 298 Calories| Fat: 33g| Protein: 3g| Carbohydrates: 4g

Cumin Mushrooms

 Prep Time: 10 minutes  Cook Time: 10 minutes   Servings: 3

Directions

1. Start sautéing the mushrooms in the butter and oil in a skillet over medium-high heat.
2. When they've gone limp and changed color, stir in the cumin and pepper.
3. Let the mushrooms cook with the spices for a minute or two, then stir in the sour cream. Cook just long enough to heat through and serve.

Nutrition: 93 Calories| Fat: 8g| Protein: 2g| Carbohydrates: 4g

Ingredients

- Eight ounces of sliced mushrooms
- One and a half tablespoons of butter
- One and a half tablespoons of olive oil
- One teaspoon of ground cumin
- A quarter teaspoon of ground black pepper
- Two tablespoons of sour cream

Dragon's Teeth

Ingredients

- One head napa cabbage
- A quarter cup of chili garlic paste
- Two tablespoons of soy sauce
- Two teaspoons of dark sesame oil
- One teaspoon of salt
- Twelve drops of liquid stevia (plain)
- Two tablespoons of peanut or canola oil
- Two teaspoons of rice vinegar

 Prep Time: 10 minutes   Cook Time: 15 minutes   Servings: 4

Directions

1. Cut the head of napa cabbage in half lengthwise, then lay it flat side down on the cutting board and slice it about Half-inch (1 cm) thick. Cut it one more time, lengthwise down the middle, and then do the other half head.
2. Mix together the chili garlic paste, soy sauce, sesame oil, salt, and stevia in a small dish, and set by the stove.
3. In a wok or extra-large skillet, over the highest heat, heat the peanut or canola oil. Add the cabbage and start stir-frying.
4. After about a minute, add the seasoning mixture and keep stir-frying until the cabbage is just starting to wilt—you want it still crispy in most places.
5. Sprinkle in the rice vinegar, stir once more, and serve.

Nutrition: 175 Calories| Fat: 9g| Protein: 0g| Carbohydrates: 3g

Japanese Fried Rice

 Prep Time: 10 minutes  Cook Time: 15 minutes   Servings: 5

Directions

1. Turn your cauliflower into Cauli-Rice according to the instructions provided in the vegetable and side recipes (Chapter 11).
2. While that's happening, whisk the eggs, pour them into a non-stick skillet (or one you've coated with non-stick cooking spray), and cook over medium-high heat. As you cook the eggs, use your spatula to break them up into pea-sized bits.
3. Remove from the skillet and set aside.
4. Remove the tips and strings from the snow peas and snip them into 1/4-inch (6 mm) lengths. (By now, the microwave has beeped—take the lid off your cauliflower, or it will turn into a mush that bears not the slightest resemblance to rice!)
5. Melt the butter in the skillet and sauté the pea pods, onion, and carrot for 2 to 3 minutes. Add the cauliflower and stir everything together well.
6. Stir in the soy sauce and cook the whole thing, often stirring, for another 5 to 6 minutes. Add a little salt and pepper and serve.

Nutrition: 91 Calories| Fat: 6g| Protein: 4g| Carbohydrates: 5g

Ingredients

- Half head cauliflower
- Two eggs
- One cup of fresh snow pea pods
- Two tablespoons of butter
- Half cup of diced onion
- Two tablespoons of shredded carrot
- Three tablespoons of soy sauce
- Salt and ground black pepper to taste

Lemon-Herb Zucchini

 Prep Time: 10 minutes   Cook Time: 15 minutes   Servings: 4

Directions

1. Cut your zukes in half lengthwise, then slice them 1/4 inch (6 mm) thick.
2. Coat your large, heavy skillet with non-stick cooking spray, and put over medium-high heat.
3. Add the olive oil. When it's hot, add your sliced zucchini, and sauté, frequently stirring, till it's just softening.
4. Add the lemon juice, coriander, thyme, and garlic. Stir everything together, reduce the heat to medium-low, and let it simmer for another few minutes.
5. Stir in the parsley just before serving.

Nutrition: 78 Calories| Fat: 7g| Protein: 1g| Carbohydrates: 4g

Ingredients

- Two medium zucchini
- Two tablespoons of olive oil
- Two tablespoons of lemon juice
- Half teaspoon of ground coriander
- A quarter teaspoon of dried thyme
- One clove of garlic, minced
- Two tablespoons of chopped fresh parsley

Mushroom Risotto

 Prep Time: 10 minutes  Cook Time: 20 min   Servings: 5

Directions

1. While the cauliflower is cooking, melt the butter in a large skillet over medium-high heat.
2. Add the mushrooms, onion, and garlic, and sauté them all together.
3. When the cauliflower is done, pull it out of the microwave and drain it. When the mushrooms have changed color and are looking done, add the cauliflower to the skillet and stir everything together.
4. Stir in the vermouth and bouillon, add the cheese, and let the whole thing cook for another 2 to 3 minutes.
5. Sprinkle just a little guar or xanthan over the "risotto," stirring all the while to give it a creamy texture.
6. Stir in the parsley just before serving.

Nutrition: 139 Calories| Fat: 11g| Protein: 6g| Carbohydrates: 4g

Ingredients

- Half head cauliflower
- Three tablespoons of butter
- One cup of sliced mushrooms
- Half medium onion, diced
- One teaspoon of minced garlic or two cloves of garlic minced
- Two tablespoons of dry vermouth
- One tablespoon of chicken bouillon concentrate
- 3/4 cup of grated Parmesan cheese
- Guar or xanthan, as needed
- Two tablespoons of chopped fresh parsley

Mushrooms with Bacon, Sun-Dried Tomatoes, and Cheese

Ingredients

- Four slices of bacon
- Eight ounces of sliced mushrooms
- Half teaspoon of minced garlic or one clove of fresh garlic, minced
- A quarter cup of diced sun-dried tomatoes—about ten pieces before dicing
- Two tablespoons of heavy cream
- 1/3 cup of shredded Parmesan cheese

 Prep Time: 10 minutes   Cook Time: 30 minutes   Servings: 4

Directions

1. Chop up the bacon or snip it up with kitchen shears. Start cooking it in a large, heavy skillet over medium-high heat. As some grease starts to cook out of the bacon, stir in the mushrooms.
2. Let the mushrooms cook until they start to change color and get soft. Stir in the garlic and cook for 4 to 5 more minutes.
3. Stir in the tomatoes and cream and cook until the cream is absorbed.
4. Scatter the cheese over the whole thing, stir it in, let it cook for just another minute, and serve.

Nutrition: 113 Calories| Fat: 8g| Protein: 6g| Carbohydrates: 5g

Pepperoncini Spinach

Prep Time: 10 minutes

Cook Time: 12 minutes

Servings: 3

Directions

1. Put your thawed spinach in a strainer, and either press it with the back of a spoon or actually pick it up with clean hands and squeeze it—you want all the excess water out of it.
2. Give your medium skillet a shot of non-stick cooking spray, put it over medium-high heat, and add the olive oil.
3. When it's hot, add spinach, pepperoncini, and garlic.
4. Sauté, often stirring, for about 5 minutes. Stir in the lemon juice, let it cook another minute, and serve.

Nutrition: 47 Calories| Fat: 3g| Protein: 5g| Carbohydrates: 5g

Ingredients

- One package of (10 ounces) frozen chopped spinach, thawed
- One and a half teaspoons of olive oil
- Two pepperoncini peppers, drained and minced
- One clove of garlic
- One tablespoon of lemon juice

Sautéed Mushrooms and Spinach with Pepperoni

Ingredients

- One ounce of sliced pepperoni
- Two tablespoons of olive oil, divided
- One pound of sliced mushrooms
- One bunch of scallions, sliced
- Two cloves of garlic, crushed
- One bag of (5 ounces) baby spinach
- Salt and ground black pepper to taste

Prep Time: 10 minutes

Cook Time: 20 minutes

Servings: 6

Directions

1. Slice your pepperoni into teeny strips.
2. Heat One tablespoon of the olive oil in your large, heavy skillet, add the pepperoni, and sauté it until it's crisp. Lift out with a slotted spoon and drain on paper towels.
3. Add the remaining One tablespoon of oil to the skillet, and let it heat over a medium-high burner.
4. Add the mushrooms and sauté them until they've softened and started to brown.
5. Add the sliced scallions and sauté for another few minutes until they're starting to brown, too. Stir in the garlic, then add the spinach.
6. Turn the whole thing over and over, just until the spinach wilts. Stir in the pepperoni bits, season with salt and pepper to taste, and serve.

Nutrition: 298 Calories| Fat: 33g| Protein: 3g| Carbohydrates: 4g

Sweet-and-Sour Cabbage

 Prep Time: 10 minutes  Cook Time: 18 minutes Servings: 4

Directions

1. In a heavy skillet, cook the bacon until crisp. Remove and drain.
2. Add the cabbage to the bacon grease and sauté it until tender-crisp, about 10 minutes.
3. Stir together the vinegar and stevia. Stir this into the cabbage. Crumble in the bacon just before serving so it stays crisp.

Nutrition: 46 Calories| Fat: 3g| Protein: 2g| Carbohydrates: 4g

Ingredients

- Three slices of bacon
- Four cups of shredded cabbage
- Two tablespoons of cider vinegar
- Twelve drops of liquid stevia (English toffee)

Two-Cheese Cauliflower

 Prep Time: 10 minutes Cook Time: 15 minutes Servings: 8

Directions

1. Preheat the oven to 350°F,
2. Lightly coat a 2-quart baking dish with non-stick cooking spray.
3. Put the cauliflower florets in a microwavable casserole dish, add Two tablespoons of water (28 ml), and cover.
4. Microwave it for 10 to 11 minutes, or until very tender.
5. Stir two tablespoons of poppy seeds into the cauliflower before baking. This gives it a kind of polka-dot look and adds subtle sophistication to the flavor.

Nutrition: 213 Calories| Fat: 17g| Protein: 13g| Carbohydrates: 3g

Ingredients

- One head of cauliflower, cut into florets (One and a half pounds of frozen cauliflower)
- One large egg
- One cup of small-curd whole-milk cottage cheese
- One cup of sour cream
- Half teaspoon of salt
- 1/8 teaspoon of ground black pepper
- Eight ounces of sharp Cheddar cheese, shredded
- Two tablespoons of chopped fresh parsley (optional)

Grains, Beans, and Legumes Recipes

Avocado and Brown Rice Salad

Ingredients

- Six ounces of brown basmati rice
- Ten ounces of skinless roast chicken, diced
- Two ripe avocados, peeled, stoned, and diced
- Six spring onions, finely sliced
- Nine ounces of cherry tomatoes, cut in half
- A pinch of red pepper flakes (optional)
- Salt and freshly ground black pepper

For the dressing
- Three tablespoons of olive oil
- One tablespoon of balsamic vinegar
- One small garlic clove, crushed

 Prep Time: 15 minutes  Cook Time: 35 minutes Servings: 4

Directions

1. Cook the rice in a pan of boiling water according to the instructions on the package. Once the rice is cooked, drain well and allow to cool.
2. To make the dressing, combine the oil, vinegar, and garlic.
3. Transfer the rice to a serving bowl, and stir in the chicken, avocado, spring onions, tomatoes, and red pepper flakes, if using. Pour the dressing over the salad and serve immediately.

Nutrition: 511 Calories| Fat: 26g| Protein: 12g| Carbohydrates: 40g

Balsamic Green Beans with Bacon and Pine Nuts

Ingredients

- Two slices of bacon
- One pound of frozen green beans, French cut
- A quarter medium onion
- One tablespoon of olive oil
- One teaspoon of butter
- One teaspoon of dried marjoram
- A quarter cup of pine nuts, toasted
- Two tablespoons of balsamic vinegar

 Prep Time: 10 minutes Cook Time: 20 minutes Servings: 8

Directions

1. First, lay your bacon on a microwave bacon rack or on a glass pie plate. Nuke it for 2 minutes on high or until crisp. Remove from the microwave, drain, and reserve.
2. While the bacon's cooking, put your green beans, still frozen, in a microwavable casserole dish with a lid.
3. Add a couple of tablespoons (30 ml) of water, cover, and when the bacon is done, put them in the microwave for 7 minutes on high.
4. Cut up your onion; you want it finely minced. Now coat your big skillet with non-stick cooking spray, put it over medium heat, and add olive oil and butter. When the butter's melted, swirl it into the olive oil, then add the onion.
5. Sauté for just a few minutes till the onion is translucent. Stir in the marjoram. Turn off the heat if the beans aren't done yet—it's better than burning your onion!
6. When the microwave beeps, stir your green beans and give them three more minutes. You want them tender but not overcooked.
7. (If your pine nuts aren't toasted, you'll need to do that, too. Spread them in a shallow pan and give them 7 or 8 minutes at 325°F -you want them just turning golden.
8. Okay, your beans are done. Drain them and throw them in the skillet with the onion—if you've turned off the heat, turn it back on to medium-high. Stir it up.
9. Now crumble the reserved bacon into the skillet, sprinkle the pine nuts over everything, and stir it up again.
10. Add the balsamic vinegar, stir one more time, and serve.

Nutrition: 73 Calories| Fat: 5g| Protein: 3g| Carbohydrates: 5g

Black Bean Soup

 Prep Time: 10 minutes Cook Time: 20 minutes Servings: 2 to 4

Directions

1. Place coconut oil, onion, carrot, and bell pepper in a stockpot.
2. Cook the veggies until tender. Bring broth to a boil. Add cooked beans, broth, and the remaining ingredients (except tapioca flour and two tablespoons of water) to the vegetables.
3. Bring that mixture to a simmer and cook for approximately 15 minutes.
4. Puree 1 quart of the soup in a blender and put it back into the pot.
5. Combine the tapioca flour and two tablespoons of water in a separate bowl.
6. Add the tapioca flour mixture to the bean soup and bring to a boil for 1 minute.

Nutrition: 132 Calories| Fat: 7g| Protein: 5g| Carbohydrates: 7g

Ingredients

- One tablespoon of Coconut Oil
- A quarter cup of Onion, Diced
- A quarter cup of Carrots, Diced
- A quarter cup of Green Bell Pepper, Diced
- One cup of beef broth
- One pound of cooked Black Beans
- One tablespoon of lemon juice
- One teaspoon of chopped Garlic
- One teaspoon of Salt
- A quarter teaspoon of Black Pepper, Ground
- One teaspoon of Chili Powder
- Four ounces of pork
- One tablespoon of tapioca flour
- Two tablespoons of Water

Frijoles Charros

 Prep Time: 10 minutes  Cook Time: 5 hour 10 minutes Servings: 4

Directions

1. Place pinto beans in a slow cooker. Cover with water. Mix in garlic and salt. Cover, and cook for 1 hour on High.
2. Cook the pork in a skillet over high heat until brown. Drain the fat.
3. Place onion in the skillet. Cook until tender. Mix in jalapenos and tomatoes. Cook until heated through.
4. Transfer to the slow cooker and stir into the beans.
5. Continue cooking for 4 hours on Low.
6. Mix in cilantro about half an hour before the end of the cooking time.

Nutrition: 237 Calories| Fat: 13g| Protein: 23g| Carbohydrates: 8g

Ingredients

- Half pound of dry pinto beans
- One clove of garlic, chopped
- Half teaspoon of salt
- A quarter-pound of pork, diced
- Half onion, chopped
- Two fresh tomatoes, diced
- Few sliced jalapeno peppers
- A quarter cup of chopped cilantro

Garbanzo Stir Fry

Ingredients

- Two tablespoons of coconut oil
- One tablespoon of oregano
- One tablespoon of chopped basil
- One clove of garlic, crushed
- Ground black pepper to taste
- Two cups of cooked garbanzo beans
- One large zucchini, halved and sliced
- Half cup of sliced mushrooms
- One tablespoon of chopped cilantro
- One tomato, chopped

 Prep Time: 10 minutes Cook Time: 30 minutes Servings: 2

Directions

1. Heat oil in a skillet over medium heat.
2. Stir in oregano, basil, garlic, and pepper. Add the garbanzo beans and zucchini, stirring well to coat with oil and herbs.
3. Cook for 10 minutes, stirring occasionally.
4. Stir in mushrooms and cilantro; cook 10 minutes, stirring occasionally.
5. Place the chopped tomato on top of the mixture to steam.
6. Cover and cook for 5 minutes more.

Nutrition: 137 Calories| Fat: 4g| Protein: 2g| Carbohydrates: 5g

Three-grain salad

Ingredients

- Five and a half ounces of brown rice
- Four and a half ounces of bulgur wheat
- Four and a half ounces of couscous
- Four tomatoes, diced
- Half cucumber, peeled and diced
- One and 3/4 ounces of fresh mint, finely chopped
- One and 3/4 ounces of fresh parsley, finely chopped
- One ounce of raisins
- Salt and freshly ground black pepper

 Prep Time: 5 minutes  Cook Time: 35 minutes  Servings: 6

Directions

1. Cook the rice in a pan of salted water for about 35 minutes until tender, or follow the instructions on the package. Drain and set aside to cool.
2. Put the bulgur wheat into a bowl and pour boiling water over it until it is just covered. Leave to stand for 5 minutes while you prepare the couscous in another bowl in the same way; leave this also for 5 minutes. Fluff up both the grains with a fork and then mix them together with the rice.
3. Stir the tomatoes, cucumber, herbs, and raisins into the grain mixture. Taste and then season if needed.

Nutrition: 381 Calories| Fat: 2g| Protein: 2g| Carbohydrates: 71g

Braised Green Beans with Pork

Ingredients

- Two cups of fresh or frozen green beans
- One onion, finely chopped
- Two cloves of garlic, thinly sliced
- A half-inch of peeled/sliced fresh ginger
- Half teaspoon of red pepper flakes, or to taste
- Two tomatoes, roughly chopped
- Two tablespoons of coconut oil
- One cup of chicken broth
- Salt and ground black pepper
- A quarter lemon, cut into wedges, to serve
- Ten ounces of lean pork

 Prep Time: 10 minutes Cook Time: 20 minutes Servings: 4

Directions

1. Cut each bean in half.
2. Heat the coconut oil in a skillet over medium heat.
3. Sauté the onion, garlic, and ginger over medium heat until they are soft.
4. Add the red pepper and tomatoes and sauté until the tomato begins to break down.
5. Stir in the green beans. Add cubed lean pork.
6. Add broth and bring to a simmer over medium heat. Cover and cook for so long that the beans get tender.
7. Season to taste with salt and pepper.
8. Serve with a wedge of lemon on the side

Nutrition: 217 Calories| Fat: 11g| Protein: 22g| Carbohydrates: 9g

Goulash

 Prep Time: 10 minutes  Cook Time: 15 min Servings: 4

Directions

1. Brown the ground beef and onion in a skillet over medium heat.
2. Drain off the fat. Add garlic, salt, and pepper to taste.
3. Stir in the cauliflower, kidney beans, and tomato paste.
4. Cook until cauliflower is done

Nutrition: 77 Calories| Fat: 6g| Protein: 2g| Carbohydrates: 5g

Ingredients

- One and a half cups of cauliflower
- Half pound of ground beef
- One small onion, chopped
- Salt to taste
- Ground black pepper to taste
- Garlic to taste
- Half cup of cooked kidney beans
- Half cup of tomato paste

Hazelnut Green Beans

 Prep Time: 10 minutes Cook Time: 15 minutes Servings: 8

Directions

1. Put your green beans in a microwaveable casserole dish with a lid, add a couple of tablespoons (30 ml) of water and nuke on high for 7 minutes.
2. In the meanwhile, chop your hazelnuts. Put your big, heavy skillet over medium heat, add the olive oil, and sauté the hazelnuts till they're touched with gold and smell wonderful. Remove from the heat.
3. By now, the microwave has beeped. Stir your beans and give them another 3 to 4 minutes.
4. When your beans are tender-crisp, drain and add to the skillet along with the lemon juice. Toss everything together, season with salt and pepper to taste, and serve.

Nutrition: 77 Calories| Fat: 6g| Protein: 2g| Carbohydrates: 5g

Ingredients

- One pound of frozen green beans
- A quarter cup of hazelnuts
- Two tablespoons of olive oil
- Two tablespoons of lemon juice
- Salt and ground black pepper to taste

Hummus

 Prep Time: 15 minutes   Cook Time: 0 minutes   Servings: 2 to 4

Directions

1. Combine tahini and lemon juice and blend for 1 minute.
2. Add the olive oil, minced garlic, cumin, and salt to the tahini and lemon mixture. Process for 30 seconds, scrape sides, and then process 30 seconds more.
3. Add half of the chickpeas to the food processor and process for 1 minute. Scrape sides, add remaining chickpeas, and process for 1 to 2 minutes.
4. Transfer the hummus into a bowl, then drizzle about One tablespoon of olive oil over the top and sprinkle with paprika

Nutrition: 187 Calories| Fat: 4g| Protein: 2g| Carbohydrates: 5g

Ingredients

- Half cup of cooked chickpeas (garbanzo beans)
- Half small lemon
- Two tablespoons of tahini
- Half of a garlic clove, minced
- One tablespoon of olive oil or cumin oil, plus more for serving
- Half teaspoon of salt
- A quarter teaspoon of ground cumin
- Two to three tablespoons of water
- Dash of ground paprika for serving

Kale White Bean Pork Soup

Ingredients

- One tablespoon of each extra-virgin olive oil and coconut oil
- One tablespoon of chili powder
- Half a tablespoon of hot jalapeno sauce
- Half pound of bone-in pork chops
- Salt
- Two stalks of celery, chopped
- One small white onion, chopped
- Two cloves of garlic, chopped
- One cup of chicken broth
- One cup of diced tomatoes
- Half cup of cooked white beans
- Two cups of packed Kale

 Prep Time: 10 minutes   Cook Time: 30 minutes   Servings: 4

Directions

1. Preheat the broiler. Whisk hot sauce, one tablespoon of olive oil, and a pinch of chili powder in a bowl. Season the pork chops with half a teaspoon of salt.
2. Rub chops with the spice mixture on both sides and place them on a rack set over a baking sheet. Set aside.
3. Heat one tablespoon of coconut oil in a large pot over high heat. Add the celery, garlic, onion, and the remaining chili powder. Cook until onions are translucent, stirring (approx. 8 minutes).
4. Add tomatoes and chicken broth to the pot. Cook and occasionally stir until reduced by about one-third (approx. 7 minutes).
5. Add the kale and the beans. Reduce the heat to medium, cover, and cook until the kale is tender (approx. 7 minutes).
6. Add up to 1/2 cup water if the mixture looks dry, and season with salt. In the meantime, boil the pork until browned (approx. 4 to 6 minutes). Flip and broil until cooked through.
7. Serve with the kale and beans

Nutrition: 213 Calories| Fat: 7g| Protein: 15g| Carbohydrates: 8g

Minestrone

Prep Time: 10 minutes Cook Time: 45 min Servings: 4

Directions

1. Heat coconut oil over medium heat in a stockpot, and sauté garlic for a few minutes.
2. Add onion and sauté for a few more minutes. Add celery and carrots and sauté for 2 minutes.
3. Stir in chicken broth, tomato sauce, and water and bring to boil, stirring frequently. Add red wine at this point.
4. Lower heat and add kidney beans, spinach leaves, green beans, zucchini, oregano, salt, basil, and pepper.
5. Simmer for 30 to 40 minutes.

Nutrition: 187 Calories| Fat: 6g| Protein: 12g| Carbohydrates: 6g

Ingredients

- One tablespoon of coconut oil
- Two cloves of garlic, chopped
- Half onion, chopped
- Half cup of chopped celery
- Two carrots, sliced
- One cup of chicken broth
- Half a cup of water
- One cup of tomato sauce
- A half-ounce of red wine (optional)
- Half cup of cooked kidney beans
- Half cup of green beans
- Half cup of baby spinach, rinsed
- One small zucchini, quartered and sliced
- Half a tablespoon of chopped oregano
- One tablespoon of chopped basil
- Salt and pepper to taste
- Half a tablespoon of olive oil or cumin oil

Sautéed Sesame Spinach

Prep Time: 10 minutes Cook Time: 12 minutes Servings: 4

Directions

1. Put the sesame seeds in a small, heavy skillet over medium-high heat, and stir or shake them until they're golden brown and toasty. Remove from the heat and reserve.
2. If you have a wok, use it for this dish. If not, coat your large, heavy skillet with non-stick cooking spray. Either way, put the pan over high heat and add the oil. When the oil is hot, add the spinach, and stir-fry till it's just barely wilted.
3. Stir in the soy sauce, and transfer to serving plates.
4. Sprinkle 3/4 teaspoon of the toasted sesame seeds on each serving and serve.

Nutrition: 72 Calories| Fat: 5g| Protein: 4g| Carbohydrates: 5g

Ingredients

- One tablespoon of sesame seeds
- One tablespoon of coconut oil or peanut oil
- One pound of fresh spinach
- Two tablespoons of soy sauce

Beef, Pork, and Lamb Recipes

Banh mi Burgers

 Prep Time: 10 minutes   Cook Time: 35 minutes   Servings: 3

Directions

1. Preheat an electric tabletop grill. If you can choose temperature settings on yours, use 350°F.
2. Cut the root and any limp greens off the scallions, whack them into a few pieces, and throw three of them into your food processor with the S-blade in place. (Reserve the other two.) Throw in the basil, too. Pulse until they're finely chopped together.
3. Now add the pork, fish sauce, chili garlic sauce, Splenda, garlic, salt, and pepper to the processor and run it until everything is well blended.
4. Form the pork mixture into three patties and put them on the grill. Set a timer for 6 to 8 minutes.
5. Quickly wash out your food processor and reassemble with the S-blade in place. Put the remaining two scallions in there and pulse to chop. Now add the mayonnaise and chili sauce and run to blend.
6. When the burgers are done, serve with the sauce.

Nutrition: 597 Calories| Fat: 32g| Protein: 19g| Carbohydrates: 7g

Ingredients

- Five scallions, divided
- A quarter cup of fresh basil leaves
- One pound of ground pork
- One tablespoon of fish sauce (nam pla or nuoc mam)
- One tablespoon of chili garlic sauce (sometimes called Sambal Oelek)
- One tablespoon of Splenda, or the equivalent in liquid Splenda
- Two teaspoons of chopped garlic
- One teaspoon of salt
- One teaspoon of ground black pepper
- 1/3 cup of mayonnaise
- One tablespoon of chili garlic sauce

Beef and Bacon Rice with Pine Nuts

Ingredients

- Half head cauliflower
- Four strips bacon
- Half medium onion, chopped
- Two tablespoons of tomato sauce
- One tablespoon of beef bouillon concentrate
- Two tablespoons of toasted pine nuts
- Two tablespoons of chopped fresh parsley

 Prep Time: 10 minutes   Cook Time: 22 minutes   Servings: 5

Directions

1. Turn your cauliflower into Cauli-Rice according to the instructions.
2. While that's cooking, cut the bacon into little pieces—kitchen shears are good for this—and start the little bacon bits frying in a heavy skillet over medium-high heat. When a little grease has cooked out of the bacon, throw the onion into the skillet.
3. Cook until the onion is translucent and the bacon is browned and getting crisp.
4. By now, the cauliflower should be done. Drain it and throw it in the skillet with the bacon and onion.
5. Add the tomato sauce and beef bouillon concentrate and stir the whole thing up to combine everything—you can add a couple of tablespoons (28 ml) of water, if you like, to help the liquid flavorings spread.
6. Stir in the pine nuts and parsley (you can just snip it right into the skillet with clean kitchen shears) and serve.

Nutrition: 72 Calories| Fat: 4g| Protein: 4g| Carbohydrates: 5g

Beef Stroganoff

Ingredients

 Prep Time: 10 minutes    Cook Time: 8 to 10 hours   Servings: 6

- Three pounds of beef stew meat in 1-inch (2.5 cm) cubes
- Three tablespoons of olive oil
- Two cups of sliced celery
- Four cloves of garlic
- One teaspoon of salt or Vege-Sal
- A quarter teaspoon of ground cinnamon
- A quarter teaspoon of ground cloves
- A quarter teaspoon of ground black pepper
- 1/8 teaspoon of ground allspice
- 1/8 teaspoon of ground nutmeg
- One can (Fourteen and a half ounces) of diced tomatoes
- Half cup of dry red wine

Directions

1. Put the beef in your slow cooker. Put the onion on top, then dump in the mushrooms, liquid, and all.
2. Mix the beef broth with the Worcestershire sauce, bouillon concentrate, and paprika, and pour over everything.
3. Cover and cook on low for 8 to 10 hours.
4. When ready to serve, cut the cream cheese into cubes and stir into the mixture in the slow cooker until melted.
5. Stir in the sour cream and serve.

Nutrition: 369 Calories| Fat: 17g| Protein: 44g| Carbohydrates: 5g

Bleu Burger

Ingredients

 Prep Time: 10 minutes   Cook Time: 14 minutes   Servings: 1

- Six ounces of ground chuck in a patty
- One tablespoon of crumbled blue cheese
- One teaspoon of finely minced sweet red onion

Directions

1. Cook the burger by your preferred method. When it's almost done to your liking, top with the blue cheese and let it melt.
2. Remove from the heat, put on a plate, and top with the onion.

Nutrition: 511Calories| Fat: 40g| Protein: 34g| Carbohydrates: 1g

Tokyo Ginger Pork Chops

Ingredients

 Prep Time: 10 minutes   Cook Time: 20 minutes   Servings: 2

- Twelve ounces of pork chops (2 chops, about 3/4 inch [2 cm] thick)
- Two tablespoons of soy sauce
- Two teaspoons of grated fresh ginger root
- One and a half teaspoons of dry sherry
- One tablespoon of coconut oil

Directions

1. Lay your chops in a shallow nonreactive container—a glass pie plate is great. Mix together the soy sauce, ginger, and sherry, and pour over the chops, turning them once to coat. Let them marinate for 15 to 20 minutes.
2. Coat your large, heavy skillet with non-stick cooking spray, and put it over medium-high heat. Let it get good and hot, then add the coconut oil. Swirl it around the bottom of the skillet to cover it. Now pick up your chops, let the marinade drip off (reserve the marinade), then throw them in the skillet and brown them a bit on both sides, about 5 minutes each.
3. Pour the reserved marinade over the chops, turn the burner down, and let the chops simmer for another 5 to 8 minutes, or until done through, then serve, scraping all the pan juices over them.

Nutrition: 337 Calories | Fat: 24g | Protein: 27g | Carbohydrates: 2g

Bourbon-Maple Glazed Pork Chops

Ingredients

- One tablespoon of olive oil
- Twelve ounces of pork loin chops (2 thin-cut chops)
- A quarter cup of minced onion
- One clove of garlic, crushed
- A quarter cup of chicken broth
- One and a half tablespoons of erythritol
- One tablespoon of bourbon
- Five drops of maple extract

Prep Time: 10 minutes **Cook Time:** 25 minutes **Servings:** 2

Directions

1. Coat your large, heavy skillet with non-stick cooking spray, and put it over medium-high heat. Add the oil and swirl it around to coat the bottom of the skillet.
2. \When the whole thing is hot, throw in your chops, and brown them on both sides, about 5 minutes per side.
3. Remove the chops from the skillet and turn the heat down to medium-low. Add the onion and garlic, and sauté in the residual fat for a minute.
4. Add the broth, erythritol, bourbon, and maple extract. Stir this around with your spatula, scraping up all the yummy brown bits stuck to the skillet.
5. Throw the chops back into the skillet. Turn the heat down to low and set a timer for 3 minutes.
6. When it goes off, flip the chops, and set the timer for another 3 minutes. By this time, the liquid should have cooked down and become syrupy.
7. Put the chops on serving plates and scrape the glaze with the bits of onion and garlic over them, then serve.

Nutrition: 225 Calories| Fat: 12g| Protein: 22g| Carbohydrates: 2g

Burger Scramble Florentine

Ingredients

- One and a half pounds of lean ground beef
- Half cup of finely diced onion
- One package of (10 ounces) frozen chopped spinach, thawed and drained
- Eight ounces of cream cheese softened
- Half cup of heavy cream
- Half cup of shredded Parmesan cheese
- Salt and ground black pepper to taste

Prep Time: 10 minutes **Cook Time:** 20 minutes **Servings:** 6

Directions

1. Preheat the oven to 350°F.
2. In a large ovenproof skillet, brown the ground beef and onion.
3. Add the spinach and cook through until the meat is done. Add the cream cheese, heavy cream, Parmesan, and salt and pepper to taste. Mix well, then spread evenly in the skillet.
4. Bake, uncovered, for 20 minutes or until bubbly and browned on top.

Nutrition: 544 Calories| Fat: 46g| Protein: 27g| Carbohydrates: 5g

Cauli-Bacon Dish

 Prep Time: 10 minutes  Cook Time: 15 min Servings: 5

Directions

1. Chop the bacon into small bits and start it frying in a large, heavy skillet over medium-high heat. (Give the skillet a squirt of non-stick cooking spray first.)
2. Chop the cauliflower into Half-inch (1 cm) bits. Chop up the stem, too; no need to waste it.
3. Put the chopped cauliflower in a microwavable casserole dish with a lid—or a microwave steamer if you have one—add a couple of tablespoons (28 ml) of water, cover, and microwave for 8 minutes on high.
4. Give the bacon a stir, then go back to the chopping board. Dice the pepper and onion. By now, some fat has cooked out of the bacon, and it is starting to brown around the edges. Add the pepper and onion to the skillet.
5. Sauté until the onion is translucent and the pepper is starting to get soft.
6. By then, the cauliflower should be done. Add it to the skillet without draining and stir—the extra little bit of water is going to help dissolve the yummy bacon flavor from the bottom of the skillet and carry it through the dish.
7. Stir in the olives, let the whole thing cook another minute while stirring, then serve.

Nutrition: 49 Calories| Fat: 4g| Protein: 2g| Carbohydrates: 3g

Ingredients

- Four slices of bacon
- Half head cauliflower
- Half green bell pepper
- Half medium onion
- A quarter cup of sliced stuffed olives

Easy Italian Beef

 Prep Time: 10 minutes Cook Time: 8 hours Servings: 6

Directions

1. Trim the beef of all outside fat. Heat the oil in your big, heavy skillet over medium-high heat, and brown the beef on both sides. Transfer it to your slow cooker.
2. In the skillet, mix together everything else but the final salt and pepper, scraping up the nice brown stuff, so it dissolves.
3. Pour this over the beef, cover the pot, and set the slow cooker to low.
4. Cook for 6 to 8 hours.
5. When cooking time is up, season with salt and pepper to taste.

Nutrition: 364 Calories| Fat: 28g| Protein: 25g| Carbohydrates: 1g

Ingredients

- Two pounds of beef chuck
- Two tablespoons of olive oil
- Half cup of beef broth
- One tablespoon of beef bouillon concentrate
- 3/4 teaspoon of lemon pepper
- Half a teaspoon of dried oregano
- Half teaspoon of garlic powder
- A quarter teaspoon of onion powder
- Twelve drops of liquid stevia
- Salt and ground black pepper to taste

Jakarta Steak

 Prep Time: 10 minutes Cook Time: 40 minutes Servings: 6

Directions

1. Marinate the steak in a shallow, nonreactive container—glass, microwavable plastic, or enamelware. It's easier than finding a resealable plastic bag big enough for your steak. Lay the steak in the container.
2. Now mix together everything else, pour it over the steak, and turn the steak once or twice to coat both sides. Stick it in the fridge, and let it marinate for several hours-overnight is brilliant.
3. You can grill this on your barbecue grill, or you can broil it. If you want to use charcoal, get it started a good 30 minutes before cooking time.
4. Either way, grill or broil it close to the heat, to your desired degree of doneness, basting both sides with the marinade when you turn it.
5. Let your steak rest for 5 minutes before carving and serving.
6. If you like, you can boil the remaining marinade hard for a few minutes to kill germs, then spoon just a little over each serving.

Nutrition: 315 Calories| Fat: 21g| Protein: 28g| Carbohydrates: 2g

Ingredients

- Two pounds of sirloin steak, trimmed at least one and a quarter inches (3 cm) thick
- Two tablespoons of soy sauce
- One tablespoon of lime juice
- Two teaspoons of grated fresh ginger root
- One teaspoon of ground turmeric
- One teaspoon of ground black pepper
- Two cloves of garlic, crushed
- Twelve drops of liquid stevia (plain)

Joe (Beef)

Ingredients

- One and a half pounds of ground beef
- One package of (10 ounces) frozen chopped spinach, thawed
- One medium onion
- Two cloves of garlic
- Six eggs
- Salt and ground black pepper to taste
- 1/3 cup of shredded Parmesan cheese

 Prep Time: 10 minutes Cook Time: 25 minutes Servings: 6

Directions

1. In your large, heavy skillet over medium heat, start browning and crumbling the ground beef. While that's happening, drain the spinach well, chop the onion, and crush the garlic.
2. When the ground beef is half done, add the onion and garlic, and cook until the beef is done through. Pour off the extra fat if you like. Now stir the spinach into the beef. Let the whole thing cook for maybe 5 minutes.
3. Now, mix up the eggs well with a fork, and stir them into the beef mixture. Continue cooking and stirring over low heat for a couple of minutes until the eggs are set. Season with salt and pepper to taste and serve topped with Parmesan.

Nutrition: 406 Calories| Fat: 29g| Protein: 29g| Carbohydrates: 5g

Kalua Pig with Cabbage

Prep Time: 10 minutes
Cook Time: 16 min
Servings: 8

Directions

1. Take a carving fork and stab your butt roast viciously all over. Do your best slasher movie imitation. You're making lots of holes to let the smoky flavor in.
2. Now sprinkle the salt all over the roast, hitting every bit of the surface, and rub it in a little. Do the same with the smoke flavoring.
3. Place your roast, Fat: side up, in your slow cooker, cover it, set it to low, and forget about it for a good 7 to 8 hours, minimum.
4. Then flip the roast, re-cover, and forget about it for another 7 to 8 hours.
5. About One and a half hours before serving time, chop your cabbage fairly coarsely and mince your onion.
6. Haul out your pork—it will fall apart and smell like heaven—put it in a big bowl and shred it with a fork. Scoop out a bit of the liquid from the pot to moisten the meat if it seems to need it. Then keep it somewhere warm (or you can rewarm it later in the microwave).
7. Throw the cabbage and onion in the remaining liquid and toss it to coat. Cover the pot, set the slow cooker on high, and let it cook for at least an hour—you want it wilted but still a little crunchy.
8. Serve the meat and cabbage together.

Nutrition: 384 Calories| Fat: 27g| Protein: 33g| Carbohydrates: 1g

Ingredients

- Three pounds of Boston butt pork roast
- Two teaspoons of sea salt
- One tablespoon of liquid smoke flavoring
- One head cabbage
- A quarter medium onion

Lamb Steaks with Lemon, Olives, and Capers

Prep Time: 10 minutes
Cook Time: 30 minutes
Servings: 4

Directions

1. Coat your large, heavy skillet with non-stick cooking spray and put it over medium-high heat. While it's heating, slash the edges of your lamb steaks to keep them from curling. When the skillet's hot, add the oil and throw in the steaks. You want to sear them on both sides.
2. When your steaks are browned on both sides, add the lemon juice, olives, capers, and garlic around and over the steaks.
3. Let the whole thing cook another minute or two, but don't overcook—the lamb should still be pink in the middle.
4. Season the steaks with salt and pepper, carve them into four portions, and serve with all the yummy lemon-caper-olive mixture from the skillet scraped over them.

Nutrition: 343 Calories| Fat: 26g| Protein: 24g| Carbohydrates: 1g

Ingredients

- One and a half pounds leg of lamb in steaks, 3/4 inch (2 cm) thick
- Two teaspoons of olive oil
- One tablespoon of lemon juice
- A quarter cup of chopped kalamata olives
- Two teaspoons of capers
- One clove of garlic
- Salt and ground black pepper to taste

Lamb, Feta, and Spinach Burgers

Ingredients

- One package of (10 ounces) frozen chopped spinach, thawed and drained
- A quarter cup of minced onion
- One tablespoon of lemon juice
- One teaspoon of dried basil
- A quarter teaspoon of salt or Vege-Sal
- A quarter teaspoon of ground black pepper
- One egg
- One clove of garlic, minced fine
- One and a quarter pounds of ground lamb
- Half cup of crumbled feta cheese
- A quarter cup of chopped sun-dried tomatoes
- Twelve kalamata olives, pitted and chopped

 Prep Time: 10 minutes  Cook Time: 15 minutes   Servings: 6

Directions

1. Make sure your spinach is well drained—put in a strainer and then squeeze it with clean hands.
2. Transfer it to a big bowl, and add the onion, lemon juice, basil, salt, pepper, egg, and garlic. Stir it all up until it's well blended.
3. Now add the lamb, feta, tomatoes, and olives. Use clean hands to mix everything until it's really well combined.
4. Make six burgers, keeping them at least 1 inch (2.5 cm) thick. Refrigerate them for at least 20 to 30 minutes before cooking.
5. Preheat your electric tabletop grill. Slap the burgers on the grill, and give them 6 to 8 minutes, depending on how well done you want them.
6. Cook to desired doneness and serve.

Nutrition: 352 Calories| Fat: 28g| Protein: 20g| Carbohydrates: 5g

Maple-Chipotle Glazed Pork Steaks

 Prep Time: 10 minutes   Cook Time: 18 minutes   Servings: 4

Directions

1. Put your large, heavy skillet over medium-high heat and start the pork steaks browning in the bacon grease.
2. Throw everything else in your blender or food processor and run until the chipotles and garlic are pulverized.
3. When your steaks are browned on both sides, add the glaze to the skillet and flip the steaks to coat on both sides. Cover with a tilted lid and let it cook until the steaks are done through and the glaze has cooked down a little—probably 10 minutes.
4. Serve, scraping all the glaze from the skillet over the steaks.

Nutrition: 412 Calories| Fat: 31g| Protein: 32g| Carbohydrates: 1g

Ingredients

- Two pounds of pork shoulder steaks or pork chops, no more than half an inch (1 cm) thick
- One tablespoon of bacon grease or coconut oil
- A quarter cup of erythritol
- Two teaspoons of spicy brown mustard
- Three chipotle chiles canned in adobo with One and a half teaspoons of the sauce
- Two cloves of garlic, crushed
- Six drops of maple extract

Maple-Spice Country-Style Ribs

Ingredients

- Three pounds of country-style pork ribs
- 2/3 cup of erythritol
- A quarter cup of chopped onion
- A quarter cup of chicken broth
- Two tablespoons of (28 ml) soy sauce
- Half teaspoon of ground cinnamon
- Half teaspoon of ground ginger
- Half teaspoon of ground allspice
- A quarter teaspoon of ground black pepper
- 1/8 teaspoon of cayenne
- 1/8 teaspoon of maple extract
- Three cloves of garlic, crushed

Prep Time: 10 minutes Cook Time: 9 hours Servings: 6

Directions

1. Put the country-style ribs in your slow cooker.
2. Mix together everything else and pour over the ribs.
3. Cover, and cook on low for 9 hours.

Nutrition: 383 Calories| Fat: 29g| Protein: 27g| Carbohydrates: 2g

Meatza

Prep Time: 10 minutes Cook Time: 30 minutes Servings: 6

Ingredients

- 3/4 pound of ground beef
- 3/4 pound of Italian sausage
- 1/3 cup of minced onion
- Two teaspoons of Italian seasoning or dried oregano
- One clove of garlic, crushed
- One cup of no-sugar-added pizza sauce
- Three tablespoons of grated Parmesan or Romano cheese (optional)
- Eight ounces of shredded mozzarella cheese

Directions

1. Preheat the oven to 350°F.
2. In a large bowl, with clean hands, combine the beef and sausage with the onion, Italian seasoning, and garlic. Mix well.
3. Pat this out in an even layer in a nine × 12-inch (23 × 30 cm) baking pan. Bake for 20 minutes.
4. When the meat comes out, it will have shrunk a fair amount because of the grease cooking off. Pour off the grease.
5. Spread the pizza sauce over the meat. Sprinkle the Parmesan on the sauce, if you like, and then distribute the shredded mozzarella evenly over the top. Set your broiler to high.
6. Put your Meatza 4 inches (10 cm) below the broiler.
7. Broil for about 5 minutes, or until the cheese is melted and starting to brown.

Nutrition: 527 Calories| Fat: 44g| Protein: 27g| Carbohydrates: 5g

Mediterranean Lamb Burgers

 Prep Time: 10 minutes
 Cook Time: 20 minutes
 Servings: 3

Ingredients

- A quarter medium onion
- Two tablespoons of chopped sun-dried tomatoes
- One pound of ground lamb
- One tablespoon of pesto sauce
- One tablespoon of chopped garlic
- Half teaspoon of salt or Vege-Sal
- A quarter teaspoon of ground black pepper
- Two tablespoons of pine nuts
- Three ounces of chèvre (goat cheese)

Directions

1. Preheat your electric tabletop grill to 350°F (180°C).
2. Chop your onion, and if your sun-dried tomatoes are in halves rather than prechopped, chop them up, too. Heck, even if they're prechopped, chop them a little more. Throw these things in a mixing bowl.
3. Add the ground lamb, pesto, garlic, salt, and pepper. Use clean hands to squish it all together until it's well mixed.
4. Form into three patties and throw them on the grill. Set a timer for 5 minutes.
5. While the burgers are cooking, toast your pine nuts in a dry skillet until they're touched with gold.
6. When your burgers are done, plate them, crumble an ounce of chèvre over each one, sprinkle with pine nuts, and then serve.

Nutrition: 578 Calories| Fat: 47g| Protein: 33g| Carbohydrates: 4g

Pan-Broiled Steak

 Prep Time: 10 minutes
 Cook Time: 30 minutes
 Servings: 4

Ingredients

- One and a half pounds steak, 1 inch (2.5 cm) thick—preferably rib eye, T-bone, sirloin, or strip
- One tablespoon of bacon grease or olive oil

Directions

1. Put your large, heavy skillet—cast iron is best—over the highest heat and let it get good and hot.
2. In the meantime, you can season your steak if you like (Montreal steak seasoning). Instead, you could top the finished steak with salt and pepper.
3. When the skillet's hot, add the bacon grease or oil, swirl it around, and then throw in your steak.
4. Set a timer for 5 or 6 minutes—The timing will depend on your preferred doneness and how hot your burner gets, but on my stove, 5 minutes per side with a 1-inch (2.5 cm) thick steak comes out medium-rare.
5. When the timer goes off, flip the steak and set the timer again. When the time is up, let the steak rest on a platter for 5 minutes before devouring.

Nutrition: 403 Calories | Fat: 33g | Protein: 24g | Carbohydrates: 0g

Mustard-Grilled Pork with Balsamic Onions

 Prep Time: 10 minutes   Cook Time: 15 min   Servings: 4

Directions

1. Preheat your electric tabletop grill. Spread two teaspoons of mustard on one side of the pork steaks, flip them, and spread another two teaspoons on the other side.
2. Grill for about 5 minutes, or until done through.
3. While that's happening, put your big, heavy skillet over medium-high heat, and start sautéing the onion in the olive oil.
4. Forget about tender-crisp—you want your onion soft and turning brown. When good and caramelized, stir in the balsamic vinegar. Set aside.
5. By now, your pork is done. Spread the remaining two teaspoons of mustard on the pork (an extra half teaspoon on each piece), divide the balsamic-onions mixture among the steaks, and serve.

Nutrition: 369 Calories| Fat: 29g| Protein: 29g| Carbohydrates: 4g

Ingredients

- Two tablespoons of brown mustard, divided
- One and a half pounds of boneless pork shoulder steaks (4 steaks, about half an inch [1 cm] thick)
- One large red onion, sliced thin
- One and a half tablespoons of olive oil
- One tablespoon of balsamic vinegar

Mustard-Maple Glazed Pork Steak

Ingredients

- Two pounds of pork shoulder steaks, no more than half an inch (1 cm) thick
- Salt and ground black pepper to taste
- One tablespoon of olive oil
- A quarter cup of chicken broth or a quarter teaspoon of chicken bouillon concentrate dissolved in a quarter cup of water
- One tablespoon of erythritol
- One tablespoon of spicy brown or Dijon mustard
- Five drops of maple extract

 Prep Time: 10 minutes   Cook Time: 35 minutes   Servings: 4

Directions

1. Give your large, heavy skillet a shot of non-stick cooking spray and start it heating over high heat while you season the pork steaks with salt and pepper.
2. In a minute or so, add the olive oil, swirl it around to coat the pan, and throw in your steaks.
3. Cover them with a tilted lid.
4. Mix together everything else and place it by the stove.
5. After about 5 minutes, flip your pork steaks and let them cook on the other side, again with a tilted lid.
6. When your pork steaks are almost done, transfer them to a plate.
7. Pour the mustard-maple mixture into the pan and stir it around, scraping up any tasty brown bits. Let it boil hard until it cooks down by about half.
8. Put the steaks back in, flip them to coat, and let the whole thing keep cooking just a minute more until the sauce is the consistency of half-and-half.
9. Plate the steaks, pour the sauce over them, and serve.

Nutrition: 437 Calories | Fat: 32g | Protein: 30g | Carbohydrates: 1g

Middle Eastern Marinated Lamb Kabobs

Prep Time: 20 minutes | Cook Time: 20 minutes | Servings: 4

Ingredients

- One pound of boneless leg of lamb, cubed
- A quarter cup of olive oil
- A quarter cup of lemon juice
- Four cloves of garlic, minced fine
- One medium onion
- Salt and ground black pepper to taste

Directions

1. Put your lamb cubes in a big resealable plastic bag. Mix together the olive oil, lemon juice, and garlic and pour over the lamb. Seal the bag, pressing out the air as you go.
2. Turn the bag once or twice to coat and throw it in the fridge for several hours.
3. If you plan to use bamboo skewers, put them in water to soak about 30 minutes before cooking time.
4. If you want to cook them over charcoal—get your fire going a good 30 minutes before you want to cook.
5. When dinner rolls around, cut your onion into chunks, and separate it into individual layers. Pull out your lamb cubes and pour off the marinade into a dish.
6. Thread the lamb cubes onto four skewers. Alternate your lamb chunks with pieces of onion.
7. Keep it compact, with stuff touching, not strung out. When the skewers are full and all the lamb and onion are used up, sprinkle your kabobs with a little salt and pepper.
8. Now grill or broil, occasionally basting with the reserved marinade, for 8 to 10 minutes or until done to your liking.
9. Stop basting with 3 to 4 minutes to go to make sure any of the raw meat germs in the marinade get killed. Serve one skewer per person.

Nutrition: 383 Calories| Fat: 28g| Protein: 29g| Carbohydrates: 5g

Pepperoncini Beef

Prep Time: 10 minutes | Cook Time: 8 hours | Servings: 6

Ingredients

- Three pounds of boneless chuck pot roast
- One cup of pepperoncini peppers, with the vinegar they're packed in
- Half medium onion, chopped
- Guar or xanthan
- Salt and ground black pepper to taste

Directions

1. Put the beef in the slow cooker, pour the pepperoncini on top, and strew the onion over that.
2. Put on the lid, set the slow cooker to low, and leave it for 8 hours.
3. When it's done, transfer the meat to a platter, and use a slotted spoon to fish out the peppers and pile them on top of the roast.
4. Thick the juices in the pot just a little with the guar or xanthan, season with salt and pepper to taste, and serve with the roast.

Nutrition: 325Calories | Fat: 24g | Protein: 24g | Carbohydrates: 3g

Poor Man's Poivrade

Prep Time: 10 minutes
Cook Time: 25 minutes
Servings: 1

Directions

1. Roll your raw beef patty in the pepper until it's coated all over. Fry the burger in the butter over medium heat until done to your liking.
2. Remove the hamburger to a plate.
3. Add the wine to the skillet and stir it around for a minute or two until all the nice brown crusty bits are scraped up.
4. Pour this over the hamburger and serve.

Nutrition: 587 Calories | Fat: 47g | Protein: 31g | Carbohydrates: 4g

Ingredients

- Six ounces of ground chuck in a patty half an inch (1 cm) thick
- One tablespoon of coarsely cracked pepper
- One tablespoon of butter
- Two tablespoons of dry white wine or dry sherry

Pork Loin with Red Wine and Walnuts

Prep Time: 10 minutes
Cook Time: 40 minutes
Servings: 4

Directions

1. Coat your large, heavy skillet with non-stick cooking spray, and put it over medium-high heat. When it's hot, add one tablespoon of the butter, swirl it around as it melts, then lay the pork in the skillet. Sauté until it's just golden on both sides.
2. Remove the pork from the skillet but keep it nearby.
3. Add half of the remaining butter to the skillet, and let it melt. Add the onion and sauté until it's getting limp. Spread the onion in an even layer in the skillet and lay the pork on top.
4. Mix together the wine, beef bouillon concentrate, and garlic. Pour it over the pork, cover the pan with a tilted lid (leave a 1/4-inch [6 mm] gap for steam to escape), turn the burner to low, and let the whole thing simmer for 20 minutes.
5. In the meantime, melt the remaining One and a half teaspoons of butter in a small skillet over medium heat, and stir the walnuts in it for 5 minutes until they smell a little toasty. Remove from the heat and reserve.
6. When the timer beeps, add the parsley to the skillet. Let the whole thing simmer for another 5 minutes or so.
7. Serve with the pan juices and a tablespoon of walnuts on each serving.

Nutrition: 322 Calories | Fat: 21g | Protein: 23g | Carbohydrates: 4g

Ingredients

- Two tablespoons of butter, divided
- One pound of boneless pork loin, cut into four servings
- One small onion, sliced
- Half cup of dry red wine
- Half a teaspoon of beef bouillon concentrate
- One clove of garlic, minced
- A quarter cup of chopped walnuts
- A quarter cup of chopped fresh parsley

Pork with a Camembert Sauce

Ingredients

- One pound of boneless pork loin, cut into three portions, about 3/4 inch (2 cm) thick
- Two ounces of Camembert cheese
- One tablespoon of butter
- Three tablespoons of dry white wine, or better yet, hard cider
- One tablespoon of chopped fresh sage
- 1/3 cup of sour cream
- One and a half teaspoons of Dijon mustard
- Ground black pepper to taste

 Prep Time: 10 minutes   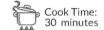 Cook Time: 30 minutes   Servings: 3

Directions

1. One at a time, put the pieces of pork loin in a heavy resealable plastic bag and pound with any handy blunt object until the meat is half an inch (1 cm) thick.
2. Using a very sharp, thin-bladed knife, cut the rind off your Camembert as thinly as possible to leave as much of the actual cheese as you can. Cut the cheese into Half-inch (1 cm) chunks and reserve.
3. Coat your large, heavy skillet with non-stick cooking spray, and put it over medium-high heat. Add the butter.
4. When the butter is melted and the pan is good and hot, swirl the butter around the bottom of the skillet, then lay your pork in it.
5. Cook until lightly golden on both sides, but no more—it's easy to dry out boneless pork loin. Put the pork on a plate and keep it in a warm place.
6. Add the wine to the skillet, and stir it around with a spatula, scraping up all the flavorful brown bits.
7. Add the sage and stir again. Turn the heat down to medium-low. Now throw in those chunks of Camembert.
8. Use your spatula to stir them around and cut the chunks into smaller bits until the cheese has completely melted.
9. Whisk in the sour cream and mustard, season with pepper to taste, and it's done.

Nutrition: 333 Calories | Fat: 20g | Protein: 32g | Carbohydrates: 2g

Rib-Eye Steak with Wine Sauce

 Prep Time: 10 minutes   Cook Time: 35 minutes   Servings: 4

Ingredients

- One and a half pounds of rib-eye steak
- One tablespoon of olive oil
- Two shallots
- Half cup of dry red wine
- Half cup of beef stock or a Half teaspoon of beef bouillon concentrate dissolved in a half cup of water
- One tablespoon of balsamic vinegar
- One tablespoon of dried thyme
- One teaspoon of brown or Dijon mustard
- Three tablespoons of butter
- Salt and ground black pepper to taste

Directions

1. Cook your steak in olive oil as described in Pan-Broiled Steak.
2. In the meantime, assemble everything for your wine sauce—chop your shallots and combine the wine, beef stock, vinegar, thyme, and mustard in a measuring cup with a pouring lip. Whisk them together.
3. When the timer goes off, flip the steak and set the timer again.
4. When your steak is done, put it on a platter and set it in a warm place. Pour the wine mixture into the skillet and stir it around, scraping up the nice brown bits, and let it boil hard.
5. Continue boiling your sauce until it's reduced by at least half.
6. Melt in the butter, season with salt and pepper, and serve with your steak.

Nutrition: 428 Calories | Fat: 28g | Protein: 35g | Carbohydrates: 2g

Roman Lamb Steak

Ingredients

 Prep Time: 10 minutes Cook Time: 15 minutes Servings: 2

- 3/4 pound of the leg of lamb steaks, half an inch (1 cm) thick
- Half cup of chopped fresh parsley
- One tablespoon of olive oil
- One tablespoon of lemon juice
- A quarter teaspoon of ground black pepper
- 1/8 teaspoon of salt
- Two anchovy fillets
- One clove of garlic, crushed

Directions

1. Put your lamb steak on a plate. Throw everything else in your food processor with the S-blade in place and pulse to chop the parsley, anchovies, and garlic into a coarse paste.
2. Smear half of the resulting mixture on one side of the steak, turn it, and smear the rest on the other side. Now let the steak sit for at least half an hour—a couple of hours is great.
3. After marinating, preheat your broiler and broil the lamb close to the heat (with the parsley mixture still all over it) for about 6 minutes per side—it should still be pink in the middle—and serve

Nutrition: 387Calories | Fat: 30g | Protein: 26g | Carbohydrates: 2g

Sirloin with Anaheim-Lime Marinade

Ingredients

 Prep Time: 10 minutes Cook Time: 30 minutes Servings: 4

- One and a half pounds of sirloin steak, trimmed
- 1/3 cup of lime juice
- Two tablespoons of olive oil
- A quarter teaspoon of ground black pepper
- Half Anaheim chile pepper
- Two cloves of garlic

Directions

1. Put your steak in a shallow, nonreactive pan—glass or stainless steel are good—that just fits it and pierce it all over with a fork.
2. Put everything else in your food processor with the S-blade in place, and run it till the pepper and garlic are pureed.
3. Pour the marinade over the steak. Let the whole thing sit for at least half an hour, and an hour or two is great.
4. Preheat the broiler or grill. Remove the steak from the marinade, reserving the marinade. Broil or grill your steak, close to high heat, until done to your liking.
5. Baste both sides with the marinade when turning the steak over, then quit—you want the heat to kill any germs before your steak is done.
6. Let your steak rest for 5 minutes before carving and serving.

Nutrition: 415 Calories | Fat: 30g | Protein: 32g | Carbohydrates: 3g

Smothered Burgers

Ingredients

 Prep Time: 10 minutes Cook Time: 18 minutes Servings: 4

- One and a half pounds ground chuck, in 4 patties (6 ounces each)
- Two tablespoons of butter or olive oil
- Half cup of sliced onion
- Half cup of sliced mushrooms
- 1/8 teaspoon of anchovy paste
- One dash of soy sauce

Directions

1. Start cooking your burgers by your preferred method.
2. While that's happening, melt the butter in a small, heavy skillet over medium-high heat.
3. Add the onion and mushrooms and sauté until the onion is translucent. Stir in the anchovy paste and soy sauce.
4. Serve the onion-mushroom mixture over the burgers.

Nutrition: 508 Calories | Fat: 41g | Protein: 31g | Carbohydrates: 2g

Slow-Cooker Pork Chili

 Prep Time: 10 minutes

 Cook Time: 8 hours

Servings: 8

Ingredients

- One tablespoon of olive oil
- Two and a half pounds of boneless pork loin, cut into 1-inch (2.5 cm) cubes
- One can (Fourteen and a half ounces) of diced tomatoes with green chiles
- A quarter cup of chopped onion
- A quarter cup of diced green bell pepper
- One tablespoon of chili powder
- One clove of garlic, crushed
- Sour cream (optional)
- Shredded Monterey Jack cheese (optional)

Directions

1. Heat the olive oil in your big, heavy skillet, and brown the pork cubes all over. Dump them in the slow cooker.
2. Stir in the tomatoes, onion, pepper, chili powder, and garlic.
3. Cover and cook on low for 6 to 8 hours.
4. Serve with sour cream and shredded Monterey Jack, if you like, but it's darned good as is.

Nutrition: 189 Calories | Fat: 8g | Protein: 3g | Carbohydrates: 3g

Zucchini Meat Loaf Italiano

Ingredients

- Two medium zucchini, chopped—about One and a half cup
- One medium onion, chopped
- Two cloves of garlic, crushed
- Olive oil—a few tablespoons as needed
- One and a half pounds of ground chuck
- 3/4 cup of grated Parmesan cheese
- Three tablespoons of olive oil
- Two tablespoons of snipped fresh parsley
- One teaspoon of salt
- Half teaspoon of ground black pepper
- One egg

 Prep Time: 10 minutes

 Cook Time: 1 h 30 min

 Servings: 5

Directions

1. Preheat the oven to 350°F.
2. Sauté the zucchini, onion, and garlic in the olive oil for about 7 to 8 minutes. Let it cool a bit, then put it in a big bowl with the rest of the ingredients.
3. Using clean hands, mix thoroughly. This will make a rather soft mixture—you can put it in a big loaf pan if you like or form it on a broiler rack.
4. Bake for 75 to 90 minutes, or until the juices run clear, but it's not dried out.

Nutrition: 521 Calories | Fat: 41g | Protein: 31g | Carbohydrates: 5g

Spareribs Adobado

 Prep Time: 10 minutes  Cook Time: 2 h 45 min   Servings: 6

Directions

1. Preheat the oven to 325°F.
2. Crush two cloves of garlic and stir into one tablespoon of olive oil. Let it sit for 10 minutes.
3. Then use clean hands to rub this mixture all over the ribs, coating both sides. Put them in a roasting pan.
4. In a small dish, stir together the seasonings. Remove one tablespoon of the mixture to a small bowl and reserve.
5. Sprinkle the ribs all over with the seasoning mixture that you didn't reserve in the bowl. Cover all sides.
6. Put the ribs in to roast and set your timer for 25 minutes (a few minutes one way or another won't matter).
7. While the ribs are roasting, crush the last clove of garlic and add to the reserved spice mixture with the chicken broth and the remaining three tablespoons of olive oil. Stir to combine. This is your mopping sauce.
8. When the timer goes off, baste your ribs with the mopping sauce, turning them over as you do so. Stick them back in the oven and set the timer for another 20 minutes.
9. Repeat for a good one and a half to two hours; you want your ribs sizzling and brown all over and tender when you pierce them with a fork.
10. Cut into individual ribs to serve.

Nutrition: 493Calories | Fat: 43g | Protein: 25g | Carbohydrates: 2g

Ingredients

- Three cloves of garlic, divided
- Four tablespoons of olive oil, divided
- Three pounds of pork spareribs
- One tablespoon of paprika
- One teaspoon of ground cumin
- One teaspoon of dried oregano
- Half teaspoon of salt or Vege-Sal
- Half teaspoon of ground black pepper
- Half cup of chicken broth

Steak au Poivre with Brandy Cream

 Prep Time: 10 minutes   Cook Time: 35 minutes   Servings: 2

Directions

1. Place your steak on a plate, and scatter two teaspoons of the pepper evenly over it.
2. Using your hands or the back of a spoon, press the pepper firmly into the steak's surface. Turn the steak over and do the same thing to the other side with the remaining pepper.
3. Place a large, heavy skillet over high heat, and add the butter and olive oil. When the skillet is hot, add your steak. For a Half-inch (1 cm) thick steak, four and a half minutes per side is about right; go maybe a minute more for a ¾ inch (2 cm) thick steak.
4. When the steak is done on both sides, turn off the burner, pour the Cognac over the steak, and flame it. When the flames die down, remove the steak to a serving platter, and pour the cream into the skillet.
5. Stir it around, dissolving the meat juices and brandy into it.
6. Season lightly with salt and pour over the steak.

Nutrition: 557 Calories | Fat: 42g | Protein: 32g | Carbohydrates: 3g

Ingredients

- Twelve ounces of well-marbled steaks—such as sirloin, T-bone, or rib-eye— Half to 3/4 inch (1 to 2 cm) thick
- Four teaspoons of coarse cracked black pepper, divided
- One tablespoon of butter
- One tablespoon of olive oil
- Two tablespoons of Cognac or other brandy
- Two tablespoons of heavy cream
- Salt, to taste

Poultry Recipes

Balsamic-Glazed Chicken and Peppers

 Prep Time: 10 minutes   Cook Time: 30 minutes   Servings: 4

Directions

1. Cut your chicken into Half-inch (1 cm) cubes. Cut your peppers into strips, cut them thinly lengthwise, then once crosswise.
2. Cut your onion in half vertically, and slice vertically. Mince your garlic and have it standing ready, too.
3. Put your large, heavy skillet over medium-high heat. Add the olive oil, and let it get hot.
4. Now throw in the chicken, peppers, and onions, and stir-fry them until all the pink is gone from the chicken and the vegetables are starting to soften a bit.
5. Add the garlic, balsamic vinegar, and Italian seasoning; stir everything up. Let the whole thing cook, often stirring, until the vinegar has reduced and become a bit syrupy, then serve.

Nutrition: 217 Calories | Fat: 10g | Protein: 26g | Carbohydrates: 5g

Ingredients

- One pound of boneless, skinless chicken breast
- Half green bell pepper
- Half red bell pepper
- One small onion
- Two cloves of garlic, crushed
- Two tablespoons of olive oil
- Two tablespoons of balsamic vinegar
- One teaspoon of Italian seasoning

Chicken-Almond Rice

 Prep Time: 10 minutes   Cook Time: 18 minutes   Servings: 5

Directions

1. Turn your cauliflower into Cauli-Rice according to the instructions.
2. While that's cooking, sauté the onion in one tablespoon of the butter in a large, heavy skillet over medium-high heat.
3. When the cauliflower is done, pull it out of the microwave, drain it, and add it to the skillet with the onion.
4. Add the wine, chicken bouillon concentrate, and poultry seasoning, and stir. Turn the heat down to low.
5. Let that simmer for a minute or two while you sauté the almonds in the remaining tablespoon (14 g) of butter in a small, heavy skillet.
6. When the almonds are golden, stir them into the "rice" and serve.

Nutrition: 104 Calories | Fat: 9g | Protein: 2g | Carbohydrates: 4g

Ingredients

- Half head cauliflower
- Half medium onion, chopped
- Two tablespoons of butter, divided
- A quarter cup of dry white wine
- One tablespoon of chicken bouillon concentrate
- One teaspoon of poultry seasoning
- A quarter cup of sliced or slivered almonds

Chicken Breasts Stuffed with Artichokes and Garlic Cheese

Ingredients

- Four boneless, skinless chicken breasts, a total of one and a half pounds
- One jar (6 ounces) of marinated artichoke hearts, drained
- Three ounces of Boursin cheese (or similar spreadable garlic-herb cheese)
- A quarter teaspoon of ground black pepper
- Half a tablespoon of butter

 Prep Time: 10 minutes  Cook Time: 35 minutes   Servings: 4

Directions

1. Preheat the oven to 375°F.
2. One by one, place each chicken breast in a big, heavy resealable plastic bag, and seal it, pressing out the air as you go.
3. Then use any heavy, blunt implement that's handy to pound the chicken till it's ¼ inch (6 mm) thick all across. Repeat with all your chicken breasts.
4. Throw your drained artichoke hearts and your cheese in your food processor, with the S-blade in place. Add the pepper, too. Pulse until the artichokes are chopped fine but not puréed.
5. Spread one-quarter of the cheese mixture on each breast and roll up jelly-roll fashion. Hold closed with toothpicks.
6. Coat your large, heavy skillet with non-stick cooking spray, and put it over medium-high heat.
7. When it's hot, add the butter, and swirl it around to cover the bottom of the skillet. Now add your chicken rolls, and sauté till they're lightly golden, about 3 minutes per side.
8. If your skillet's handle isn't ovenproof, wrap it in foil. Slide the whole thing into the oven, and let it bake for 15 minutes, or until done through, and serve.

Nutrition: 298 Calories | Fat: 12g | Protein: 41g | Carbohydrates: 2g

Chicken Burgers with Basil and Sun-Dried Tomatoes

Ingredients

- One pound of ground chicken
- Two tablespoons of chopped dry-pack sun-dried tomatoes chopped fine
- Two tablespoons of minced onion
- One clove of garlic, minced
- One tablespoon of minced fresh basil (or one teaspoon of dried)
- One teaspoon of minced fresh oregano (or a quarter teaspoon of dried)
- One teaspoon of paprika
- Half teaspoon of salt or Vege-Sal
- A quarter teaspoon of ground black pepper
- A quarter teaspoon of cayenne

 Prep Time: 10 minutes   Cook Time: 20 minutes   Servings: 3

Directions

1. Just combine everything in a mixing bowl and use clean hands to mix it all together until it's well blended.
2. Form into three patties. If you've got a little time, put them on a plate, and chill them for 30 minutes before cooking.
3. Pan-broil these in a big, heavy skillet for about 5 to 6 minutes per side.
4. Try topping them with mayonnaise with a little lemon juice and chopped basil stirred in.

Nutrition: 345 Calories | Fat: 14g | Protein: 47g | Carbohydrates: 5g

Chicken in Creamy Horseradish Sauce

Ingredients

- Four pounds of cut-up chicken pieces
- One tablespoon of butter
- One tablespoon of olive oil
- 3/4 cup of chicken broth
- One and a half teaspoons of chicken bouillon concentrate
- One tablespoon of prepared horseradish
- Four ounces of cream cheese
- A quarter cup of heavy cream
- Guar or xanthan (optional)
- Salt and ground black pepper to taste

Prep Time: 10 minutes | Cook Time: 6 hours | Servings: 8

Directions

1. In your big, heavy skillet, over medium-high heat, brown the chicken in butter and olive oil. Transfer to slow cooker.
2. Stir together the chicken broth, bouillon concentrate, and horseradish. Pour over the chicken. Cover the pot, set the slow cooker to low, and let cook for 6 hours.
3. When time's up, fish out the chicken and put it on a platter, cut the cream cheese into chunks, and melt it into the sauce, then stir in the heavy cream. Thicken with your guar or xanthan shaker if you think it needs it.
4. Season with salt and pepper to taste and serve.

Nutrition: 442 Calories | Fat: 34g | Protein: 30g | Carbohydrates: 1g

Chicken in Creamy Orange Sauce

Ingredients

- Four pounds of skinless chicken thighs
- Three tablespoons of oil
- Half cup of white wine vinegar
- Half a cup of lemon juice
- Three tablespoons of brandy
- One teaspoon of grated orange zest
- Half teaspoon of orange extract
- A quarter teaspoon of liquid stevia (lemon drop)
- Eight scallions, sliced
- Six ounces of cream cheese
- Salt and ground black pepper to taste

Prep Time: 10 minutes | Cook Time: 6 hours | Servings: 8

Directions

1. In your big, heavy skillet, over medium-high heat, brown the chicken in the oil all over. Transfer to your slow cooker.
2. Stir together the white wine vinegar, lemon juice, brandy, orange zest, orange extract, and stevia. Pour over the chicken.
3. Cover the pot, set the slow cooker to low, and cook for 6 hours.
4. When cooking time is up, transfer the chicken to a platter. Add the sliced scallions to the liquid in the pot, then add the cream cheese, cut into chunks, and stir till it's melted.
5. Season with salt and pepper. Serve the sauce over the chicken.

Nutrition: 384 Calories | Fat: 24g | Protein: 34g | Carbohydrates: 4g

Chicken Skewers Diavolo

 Prep Time: 10 minutes  Cook Time: 35 minutes Servings: 6

Ingredients

- Two pounds of boneless, skinless chicken thighs
- A quarter cup of olive oil
- A quarter cup of lemon juice
- Two cloves of garlic, minced
- Two tablespoons of red pepper flakes
- Salt and ground black pepper to taste
- Fresh parsley, for garnish, if desired
- One lemon, cut into six wedges

Directions

1. Cut your chicken into 1-inch (2.5 cm) cubes. Put them in a big resealable plastic bag. Combine the olive oil, lemon juice, garlic, red pepper flakes, and salt and pepper, and pour over the chicken. Seal the bag, pressing out the air as you go.
2. Turn to coat, then throw the bag in the fridge, and let the chicken marinate for at least 4 to 5 hours, and all day won't hurt a bit.
3. If you're going to use bamboo skewers, put them in water to soak them 30 minutes before cooking time.
4. When the cooking time comes, preheat your grill or broiler and pour off the marinade into a dish, and reserve.
5. Thread the chicken chunks onto six skewers. You can now grill them or broil them for about 8 minutes, or until done through (cut into a chunk to see), often basting with the reserved marinade—but stop basting with at least a couple of minutes cooking time to go, to be sure all the raw chicken germs are killed.
6. Garnish each skewer with a little minced parsley, if using, and serve with a lemon wedge to squeeze over it.

Nutrition: 246 Calories | Fat: 17g | Protein: 22g | Carbohydrates: 2g

Cranberry-Peach Turkey Roast

 Prep Time: 10 minutes Cook Time: 7 hours Servings: 8

Ingredients

- Three pounds of turkey roast
- Two tablespoons of oil—light olive oil or MCT oil
- One cup of cranberries
- Half cup of chopped onion
- A quarter cup of erythritol
- Three tablespoons of spicy mustard
- A quarter teaspoon of red pepper flakes
- One peach, peeled and chopped

Directions

1. If your turkey roast is like mine (a Butterball), it will be a boneless affair of light and dark meat rolled into an oval roast, enclosed in a net sack. Leave it in the net for cooking, so it doesn't fall apart on you.
2. Heat the oil in your big, heavy skillet, and brown the turkey roast on all sides. Transfer it to a slow cooker.
3. Put the cranberries, onion, erythritol, mustard, red pepper flakes, and chopped peach in your blender or in your food processor with the S-blade in place. Run it until you have a coarse puree. Pour this over the roast.
4. Cover the slow cooker, set it to low, and let it cook for 6 to 7 hours.
5. Remove the roast to a platter and stir up the sauce.
6. Transfer the sauce to a sauceboat to serve with the turkey. You can remove the net from the turkey before serving if you like, but it's recommended to use a good sharp knife to slice clear through the netting and let each diner remove their own.

Nutrition: 255 Calories | Fat: 8g | Protein: 31g | Carbohydrates: 1g

Creamy Chicken and Noodles in a Bowl

 Prep Time: 10 minutes   Cook Time: 25 minutes   Servings: 1

Directions

1. Snip open the packet of shirataki, drain and rinse them, and throw them in a microwavable bowl. Nuke them on high for 2 minutes.
2. While that's happening, drain and dice your roasted red peppers.
3. When the microwave beeps, drain the shirataki again. Put them back in for another 2 minutes.
4. Pit your kalamatas—just squish them with your thumb and pick the pits out—then chop them up. Slice your scallion, including the crisp part of the green, and chop your parsley, too.
5. Drain your noodles one last time. Now add the cream cheese and chicken breast strips and nuke the mixture for just 30 more seconds.
6. When it comes out, throw in the peppers, olives, scallions, and parsley. Stir it up until the cheese melts, season with salt and pepper to taste, and devour!

Nutrition: 285 Calories | Fat: 22g | Protein: 16g | Carbohydrates: 5g

Ingredients

- One package (Eight ounces) of tofu shirataki, fettuccini width
- A quarter cup of jarred roasted red peppers
- Five kalamata olives
- One scallion
- One tablespoon of minced fresh parsley
- Three tablespoons of chive- and onion cream cheese
- Three ounces of precooked chicken breast strips
- Salt and ground black pepper to taste

Golden Triangle Chicken Kabobs

Ingredients

- One and a half pounds of boneless, skinless chicken thighs
- Two tablespoons of lemon juice
- One tablespoon of lime juice
- One shallot, minced
- Five cloves of garlic, crushed
- One tablespoon of grated fresh ginger root
- Two tablespoons of soy sauce
- Three drops of liquid stevia (plain)
- One teaspoon of ground turmeric

 Prep Time: 10 minutes   Cook Time: 25 minutes   Servings: 4

Directions

1. Cut your chicken into 1-inch (2.5 cm) cubes. This is easier if it's somewhat frozen.
2. Put your chicken cubes in a resealable plastic bag, then stir together everything else and pour it in. Seal the bag, pressing out the air as you go. Stash the bag in the fridge for at least several hours (24 hours is brilliant).
3. If you're going to be using bamboo skewers, you might put them in water to soak them now.
4. When dinnertime rolls around, preheat your broiler, or fire up your barbecue. Pull the bag out of the fridge, pour off the marinade into a small bowl, and reserve.
5. Thread your chicken cubes onto four skewers.
6. Start your skewers grilling or broiling, giving them about 5 minutes. Baste both sides of your kabobs with that reserved marinade (discard the rest of the marinade to avoid germs), turn them over, and give them another 5 minutes, or till done through.

Nutrition: 210 Calories | Fat: 3g | Protein: 40g | Carbohydrates: 3g

Lemon-Herb Chicken Breast

 Prep Time: 10 minutes  Cook Time: 30 min Servings: 3

Ingredients

- Two cloves of garlic, crushed
- Half cup of olive oil
- One pound of boneless, skinless chicken breast
- Salt and ground black pepper to taste
- One lemon
- Two tablespoons of water
- A quarter cup of minced fresh basil
- Two tablespoons of minced fresh parsley

Directions

1. Put the garlic in a measuring cup and pour the olive oil over it. Let it sit.
2. Give a skillet a squirt of non-stick cooking spray and put it over a high burner.
3. Now grab your chicken and a blunt, heavy object and pound your breast out to an even Half-inch (1 cm) thickness. Cut into three portions and season with salt and pepper on both sides.
4. Pour half of the garlicky olive oil into your now-hot skillet, swirl it around, and throw in your chicken. Cover it with a tilted lid—leave a crack—and let it cook for 3 to 4 minutes.
5. Your chicken should be golden on the bottom now; flip it! Re-cover with the tilted lid and give it another 3 to 4 minutes.
6. In the meantime, roll your lemon under your palm, pressing down firmly. This will help produce more juice. Slice your lemon in half and flick out the seeds with the tip of a knife.
7. When your chicken is golden on both sides, squeeze one of the lemon halves over it. Flip it to coat both sides, turn the burner down to medium-low, and re-cover with that tilted lid. Let it cook until it's done through.
8. Plate your chicken, and then add the water and the juice of the other lemon half to the skillet.
9. Stir it all around with a fork, scraping up the tasty brown bits, and then pour this over the chicken.
10. Top with the herbs and a drizzle of the remaining garlic olive oil, and then serve.

Nutrition: 508 Calories | Fat: 40g | Protein: 34g | Carbohydrates: 5g

Skillet Citrus Chicken

Ingredients

- One tablespoon of olive oil
- Three pounds of chicken thighs
- Half cup of chicken broth
- Two tablespoons of low-sugar orange marmalade preserves
- Two tablespoons of lemon juice
- Two tablespoons of lime juice
- Two teaspoons of brown mustard
- Eighteen drops of liquid stevia (lemon drop)
- Two cloves of garlic, crushed

 Prep Time: 10 minutes Cook Time: 30 minutes Servings: 5

Directions

1. Coat your large, heavy skillet with non-stick cooking spray, and put it over medium-high heat. When it's hot, add the olive oil, then the chicken, skin-side down.
2. Sauté until the chicken is lightly golden, then turn bone-side down. Brown for another 5 minutes or so.
3. While that's happening, stir together the chicken broth, low-sugar marmalade, lemon juice, lime juice, mustard, stevia, and garlic. When the chicken is browned, pour the broth mixture into the skillet.
4. Partially cover the skillet with a "tilted lid" and leave a crack of about 1/4 inch (6 mm) to let some steam out. Turn the burner to low and let the chicken simmer for 20 minutes.
5. When the time is up, uncover the chicken and remove it to a platter. Keep it in a warm place while you turn up the burner and boil down the sauce until it's a little syrupy.
6. Pour the sauce over the chicken and serve.

Nutrition: 499 Calories | Fat: 36g | Protein: 38g | Carbohydrates: 4g

Super-Easy Turkey Divan

Ingredients

- One pound of frozen broccoli, thawed
- One pound of roasted turkey, sliced
- One cup of grated Parmesan, divided
- One cup of mayonnaise
- One cup of heavy cream
- Two tablespoons of dry vermouth

 Prep Time: 10 minutes  **Cook Time:** 40 minutes **Servings:** 6

Directions

1. Preheat the oven to 350°F.
2. Coat an 8-inch (20 cm) square baking dish with non-stick cooking spray.
3. Cover the bottom of the pan with broccoli.
4. Cover the broccoli with slices of leftover turkey.
5. In a mixing bowl, combine all but two tablespoons of the Parmesan with the mayonnaise, cream, and vermouth.
6. Pour over the turkey and broccoli.
7. Sprinkle the remaining parmesan on top. Bake until it's getting golden, about a half-hour.

Nutrition: 614 Calories | Fat: 54g | Protein: 131g | Carbohydrates: 5g

Tandoori Chicken

Ingredients

- Five pounds of bone-in chicken thighs without skin
- One and a half cups of plain yogurt
- A quarter cup of olive oil
- Two tablespoons of grated fresh ginger root
- One tablespoon of lemon juice
- Two teaspoons of chili powder
- Two teaspoons of ground turmeric
- One teaspoon of salt or Vege-Sal
- One teaspoon of ground coriander
- Half teaspoon of ground cumin
- Half teaspoon of ground cinnamon
- Half teaspoon of ground cloves
- Four cloves of garlic
- Two bay leaves, whole

 Prep Time: 10 minutes **Cook Time:** 1 h 10 min **Servings:** 6

Directions

1. Skin the chicken if you didn't buy it that way. Put it in a nonreactive baking pan—glass or enamel are ideal, but stainless steel will do. Don't use aluminum or iron.
2. Put everything else in your blender and run it until you have a smooth sauce.
3. Pour the sauce over the chicken and use tongs to turn each piece to coat. Cover the baking pan with plastic wrap, slide it into the fridge, and let it sit for a minimum of 4 hours; a whole day is ideal.
4. Pull your chicken out of the fridge, and let it come to room temperature. Meanwhile, preheat your oven to 350°F.
5. When the oven is hot, pull the plastic wrap off the baking pan and slide it in to cook. Roast for 45 minutes to 1 hour, turning the chicken occasionally with your tongs.

Nutrition: 387 Calories | Fat: 20g | Protein: 45g | Carbohydrates: 5g

Tasty Roasted Chicken

Prep Time: 10 minutes

Cook Time: 1 h 40 min

Servings: 6

Ingredients

- One tablespoon of mayonnaise
- One whole chicken
- Salt and ground black pepper
- Paprika
- Onion powder

Directions

1. Preheat the oven to 375°F.
2. If your chicken is frozen, make sure it's completely thawed—if it's still a bit icy in the middle, run some hot water inside it until it's not icy anymore. Take out the giblets; if you've never cooked a whole chicken before, you'll find them in the body cavity.
3. Dry your chicken with paper towels and put it on a plate.
4. Scoop your mayonnaise out of the jar and into a small dish, being careful not to contaminate the jar. Using clean hands, give your chicken a nice mayo massage. Rub that chicken all over with the mayonnaise, coating every inch of the skin.
5. Sprinkle the chicken liberally with salt, pepper, paprika, and onion powder, all four equally, on all sides.
6. Put the chicken on a rack in a shallow roasting pan, and put it in the oven.
7. Leave the bird there for One and a half hours, or until the juices run clear when you stick a fork in where the thigh joins the body.
8. Remove from the oven, and let the chicken sit for 10 to 15 minutes before carving to let the juices settle.

Nutrition: 600 Calories | Fat: 44g | Protein: 48g | Carbohydrates: 1g

Thanksgiving Weekend Curry

Ingredients

- Three tablespoons of coconut oil
- Two teaspoons of garam masala
- One teaspoon of ground cinnamon
- One teaspoon of ground turmeric
- Half medium onion, chopped
- Two cloves of garlic, crushed
- One tablespoon of grated fresh ginger root
- One teaspoon of cayenne
- One can (14 fluid ounces) of unsweetened coconut milk
- 3/4 cup of chicken broth, or turkey broth, if you have it
- Four cups of diced cooked turkey
- Salt, to taste

Prep Time: 10 minutes

Cook Time: 40 minutes

Servings: 8

Directions

1. In your big, heavy skillet, over medium-low heat, melt the coconut oil. Add the garam masala, cinnamon, and turmeric, and stir for a minute or so.
2. Add the onion, and sauté until it's translucent.
3. Now add the garlic, ginger, and cayenne. Pour in the coconut milk and chicken broth. Stir it up until you've got a creamy sauce.
4. Stir in the turkey, and turn the burner to low. Let the whole thing simmer for 15 minutes or so.
5. Season with salt to taste and serve in bowls with soup spoons.

Nutrition: 349 Calories | Fat: 27g | Protein: 23g | Carbohydrates: 4g

Turkey with Mushroom Sauce

 Prep Time: 10 minutes   Cook Time: 8 hours   Servings: 8

Directions

1. In your big skillet, sauté the turkey breast in the butter till it's golden all over. Transfer to the slow cooker.
2. Sprinkle the parsley, tarragon, salt, and pepper over the turkey breast. Dump the mushrooms on top. Mix the wine and bouillon concentrate together until the bouillon dissolves, and pour it in as well. Cover the pot, and cook on low for 7 to 8 hours.
3. When it's done, fish the turkey out and put it on a platter. Transfer about half of the mushrooms to your blender, and add the liquid from the pot. Blend until mushrooms are puréed.
4. Scoop the rest of the mushrooms into the serving dish for the sauce, add the liquid, and thicken further with your guar or xanthan shaker, if needed.

Nutrition: 281 Calories | Fat: 14g | Protein: 34g | Carbohydrates: 1g

Ingredients

- Three pounds of boneless, skinless turkey breast (in one big hunk, not thin cutlets)
- Two tablespoons of butter
- A quarter cup of chopped fresh parsley
- Two teaspoons of dried tarragon
- Half teaspoon of salt or Vege-Sal
- A quarter teaspoon of ground black pepper
- One cup of sliced fresh mushrooms
- A quarter cup of dry white wine
- One teaspoon of chicken bouillon concentrate
- Guar or xanthan (optional)

Yucatán Chicken

 Prep Time: 10 minutes   Cook Time: 40 minutes   Servings: 4

Directions

1. Mix together everything but the chicken. Rub this mixture all over your chicken thighs and even up under the skin.
2. Refrigerate for several hours.
3. When cooking time comes, preheat your broiler, arrange the chicken on your broiler rack, skin-side down, and broil about 6 inches from the heat for 15 minutes or so. Turn, and give it another 10 minutes. Turn again, and give it at least another 5 minutes.
4. Now turn a piece skin-side up, and pierce it to the bone. If the juice runs clear, it's done. If it runs pink, you need to give it a little longer.
5. You can also cook this on your barbecue grill if you like. Indeed, if you want to take something along to the park or the beach to grill while you're there, do the flavoring step early in the day, marinating the chicken in a big resealable plastic bag. Then grab the bag of chicken, throw it in your cooler, and go.
6. Serve with a big green salad.

Ingredients

- One tablespoon of ground black pepper
- One tablespoon of ground allspice
- One teaspoon of dried oregano
- Half teaspoon of ground cumin
- One teaspoon of lime juice
- One teaspoon of lemon juice
- Three drops of orange extract
- Two pounds of chicken thighs

Nutrition: 389 Calories | Fat: 28g | Protein: 31g | Carbohydrates: 3g

Fish and seafood Recipes

Baked Clams

Prep Time: 10 minutes   Cook Time: 20 minutes   Servings: 6

Directions

1. Put everything but the clams through the food processor until the mixture is well blended. Now put a teaspoon of this mixture on each clam. Arrange in a baking pan. At this point, you may cover and refrigerate or even freeze them.
2. When you're ready to cook them, first let them come to room temperature. Preheat the oven to 375°F and bake for 10 minutes, then broil 4 inches (10 cm) or so from the heat for another 3 to 5 minutes, until golden.
3. Serve hot!

Nutrition: 225 Calories | Fat: 17g | Protein: 14g | Carbohydrates: 3g

Ingredients

- Half cup of butter
- A quarter cup of plain pork rind crumbs
- Two tablespoons of minced onion
- One tablespoon of minced fresh parsley
- One teaspoon of dried oregano or one tablespoon of minced fresh oregano
- Half teaspoon of Tabasco sauce, or to taste
- Four cloves of garlic, crushed
- Thirty-six clams in the shell—have the store open them up for you

Chili-Bacon Scallops

Ingredients

- Eight slices of bacon
- Two teaspoons of chili powder
- One pound of bay scallops

Prep Time: 10 minutes   Cook Time: 15 minutes   Servings: 4

Directions

1. Put your large, heavy skillet over medium heat and snip the bacon into it in bits about 1/4 inch (6 mm) wide. Let that fry.
2. Sprinkle the chili powder all over the scallops; sprinkle both sides, and then stir them up to make sure they are evenly seasoned.
3. When the bacon bits are about halfway done, add the scallops to the skillet and spread them out in a single layer. Let them cook for about 5 minutes, turning them a few times until they're done, though, and the bacon bits are crisp.
4. Serve with the bacon bits, and pour the grease over the top!

Nutrition: 117 Calories | Fat: 7g | Protein: 23g | Carbohydrates: 3g

Salmon in a Citrus Vinaigrette

 Prep Time: 10 minutes  Cook Time: 15 minutes   Servings: 4

Directions

1. Coat a big skillet with non-stick cooking spray and put it over medium heat. Throw in the coconut oil and when it's melted, swirl it around and then add the salmon.
2. While the salmon is getting a little touch of gold, throw everything else in the blender and run the thing.
3. Go back and flip your salmon. Let it get a little gold on the other side, too.
4. Add the vinaigrette mixture to the skillet and turn the burner up to medium-high. Let the whole thing cook for another 5 minutes or until the salmon is done through.
5. Plate the salmon and turn up the burner. Boil the sauce hard until it's reduced and starting to get a little syrupy. Pour over the salmon and serve.

Nutrition: 384 Calories | Fat: 25g | Protein: 34g | Carbohydrates: 5g

Ingredients

- One tablespoon of coconut oil
- One and a half pounds salmon fillet, cut into four servings
- Half cup of vinaigrette
- Half a cup of lemon juice
- Two and a half tablespoons of Splenda, or the equivalent in liquid Splenda
- Two tablespoons of lime juice
- One teaspoon of brown mustard
- One teaspoon of chili powder
- A quarter teaspoon of orange extract

Gingered Monkfish

Ingredients

- One pound of monkfish
- One tablespoon of (6 g) grated fresh ginger root
- One tablespoon of (15 g) Heinz Reduced Sugar Ketchup
- Two teaspoons of chili garlic paste or Sriracha
- Six ounces of asparagus, thin spears
- Three scallions
- One tablespoon of peanut oil, coconut oil, or MCT oil
- One teaspoon of dark sesame oil

 Prep Time: 10 minutes   Cook Time: 20 minutes   Servings: 4

Directions

1. Use a sharp knife to remove any membrane from the monkfish, then cut into thin, flat, round slices. Reserve.
2. In a small dish, stir together the ginger root, ketchup, and chili garlic paste. Brush this mixture over the monkfish slices. Let it sit for 5 minutes.
3. In the meantime, snap the ends off the asparagus where it wants to break naturally.
4. Cut the spears into 1-inch (2.5 cm) lengths on the diagonal. Slice your scallions, too, including the crisp part of the green.
5. If you've got a wok, use it for this. If not, use your large, heavy skillet, but coat it first with non-stick cooking spray. Either way, put it over high heat, and add the peanut oil.
6. Now add the monkfish with its sauce, the asparagus, and the scallion. Stir-fry very gently so as not to break up the fish.
7. Cook for about 5 minutes, or until the fish is done through and the vegetables are tender-crisp.
8. Drizzle in the sesame oil, toss gently to combine, and serve.

Nutrition: 139 Calories | Fat: 6g | Protein: 17g | Carbohydrates: 3g

Glazed Salmon

Prep Time: 10 minutes

Cook Time: 20 minutes

Servings: 4

Ingredients

- One and a half pounds salmon fillet, cut into four servings
- Three tablespoons of bacon grease, melted
- Salt and ground black pepper to taste
- Two tablespoons of brown mustard
- Two tablespoons of grated horseradish
- One tablespoon of erythritol

Directions

1. You can grill this or broil it. Either way, start your cooking device heating before you do anything else. If you're using a grill, make sure it's good and clean, so your fish won't stick.
2. Oil the grill or broiler pan.
3. Brush your fish on either side with bacon grease. Season lightly with salt and pepper. (If you're using bacon grease, you may want to skip the salt.)
4. Mix together everything else, and have it standing by.
5. Lay your fish on the broiler pan or grill, and give it 3 minutes. Flip and grill the other side for 3 minutes.
6. Now brush with the glaze, turn, and coat the other side, too. Give it another minute or so, then pull off the grill and serve with any remaining glaze. (Boil the glaze for a few minutes first to kill any germs!)

Nutrition: 297 Calories | Fat: 16g | Protein: 35g | Carbohydrates: 1g

Halibut with Lemon-Herb Sauce

Prep Time: 10 minutes

Cook Time: 15 minutes

Servings: 4

Ingredients

- Six tablespoons of lemon juice
- Five tablespoons of extra-virgin olive oil, divided
- Three tablespoons of chopped fresh basil
- Three tablespoons of chopped fresh parsley
- Salt and ground black pepper to taste
- Two and a quarter pounds of halibut fillets, in 4 servings
- Three tablespoons of chopped fresh chives
- One medium red bell pepper, sliced into rings

Directions

1. Preheat the broiler.
2. Put the lemon juice, four tablespoons of olive oil, the basil, and the parsley in your food processor with the S-blade. Pulse until puréed. Season with salt and pepper to taste.
3. Brush the halibut fillets with the remaining one tablespoon of oil, and season them lightly with salt and pepper. Broil for about 5 minutes per side, or until just opaque through.
4. Transfer to serving plates. Sprinkle the chives over the fish, spoon the sauce over that, arrange the pepper rings on top, and serve.

Nutrition: 383 Calories | Fat: 28g | Protein: 29g | Carbohydrates: 5g

Pesto Shrimp

Ingredients

- One and a half tablespoons of olive oil
- Three tablespoons of pesto sauce
- Eighteen ounces of shrimp, peeled and deveined

 Prep Time: 10 minutes  Cook Time: 15 min   Servings: 4

Directions

1. Combine the olive oil and pesto in your large, heavy skillet over medium-high heat.
2. When it's hot, throw in the shrimp and sauté them until they're pink clear through.
3. Serve with all the pesto sauce from the skillet scraped over them.

Nutrition: 237 Calories | Fat: 12g | Protein: 28g | Carbohydrates: 2g

Poached Trout with Dill

Ingredients

- Two tablespoons of dry white wine
- One tablespoon of lemon juice
- One tablespoon of snipped fresh dill weed, or one teaspoon of dried dill weed
- Twelve ounces of trout fillet
- Salt and ground black pepper to taste

 Prep Time: 10 minutes   Cook Time: 10 minutes   Servings: 2

Directions

1. In a shallow, nonreactive pan with a lid, combine the wine and lemon juice. Put over medium heat, and bring to a simmer.
2. Stir in the dill, and lay the trout fillets skin-side up in the wine–lemon juice mixture. Turn the heat down to low, cover the pan, and set a timer for 8 minutes.
3. Carefully transfer the trout fillets to 2 serving plates, turning them skin-side down in the process.
4. Pour the pan liquid over them, season lightly with salt and pepper, and serve.

Nutrition: 265 Calories | Fat: 11g | Protein: 35g | Carbohydrates: 1g

Deviled Pollock

Ingredients

- Six pollock fillets (about one pound)
- Two tablespoons of brown mustard
- Two tablespoons of prepared horseradish
- Four teaspoons of Heinz Reduced Sugar Ketchup
- Half teaspoon of Sriracha

 Prep Time: 10 minutes   Cook Time: 25 minutes   Servings: 3

Directions

1. Preheat the oven to 325°F.
2. Coat a shallow baking dish with non-stick cooking spray, and lay your fillets in it.
3. Mix together the mustard, horseradish, ketchup, and Sriracha. Spread this mixture over the fish, coating the surface evenly.
4. Bake for 20 minutes, or until the fish flakes easily, and serve.

Nutrition: 142 Calories | Fat: 2g | Protein: 27g | Carbohydrates: 2g

Salmon with Pesto Mayonnaise

 Prep Time: 10 minutes  Cook Time: 15 minutes   Servings: 4

Directions

1. Coat a shallow baking pan with non-stick cooking spray, and arrange your salmon fillets in it, skin-side down. Set the broiler for low heat, and broil the salmon about 4 inches (10 cm) from the heat source for 4 to 5 minutes.
2. Meanwhile, combine the mayonnaise and pesto sauce. When the initial broiling time is up, spread the pesto mayonnaise on the salmon. Top each serving with One tablespoon of (5 g) Parmesan.
3. Run back under the broiler for One and a half minutes, or until the cheese is lightly browned.

Nutrition: 342 Calories | Fat: 21g | Protein: 37g | Carbohydrates: 1g

Ingredients

- One and a half pounds salmon fillet, cut into four servings
- A quarter cup of mayonnaise
- Four teaspoons of pesto sauce
- Four teaspoons of shredded Parmesan cheese

Sizzling Moroccan Shrimp

 Prep Time: 10 minutes   Cook Time: 15 minutes   Servings: 3

Directions

1. Coat your large, heavy skillet with non-stick cooking spray, and put it over high heat.
2. When it's hot, add the olive oil, and throw in the shrimp. Sauté, often turning, until they're just barely pink all over.
3. Stir in the remaining ingredients, sauté another minute or so, till the shrimp are pink throughout, and serve.

Nutrition: 212 Calories | Fat: 7g | Protein: 31g | Carbohydrates: 4g

Ingredients

- One tablespoon of olive oil
- One pound of shrimp, peeled and deveined
- Two teaspoons of lemon juice
- Two teaspoons of paprika
- One teaspoon of ground cumin
- Half teaspoon of ground ginger
- 1/8 teaspoon of cayenne, or to taste
- Two cloves of garlic, minced

Sun-Dried Tomato-Portobello Salmon Roast

Prep Time: 10 minutes
Cook Time: 35 min
Servings: 2

Ingredients

- Two tablespoons of boiling water
- Two tablespoons of chopped sun-dried tomatoes
- Eight ounces of salmon fillet, in 2 pieces about the same shape
- Three teaspoons of olive oil, divided
- A quarter cup of sliced mushrooms—portobellos, the little ones
- One ounce of provolone cheese, sliced
- One teaspoon of minced fresh parsley

Directions

1. Preheat the oven to 350°F.
2. Pour the boiling water over your chopped sun-dried tomatoes. Let them sit while you use a sharp knife to remove the skin from your salmon if it has skin.
3. Coat a little skillet with non-stick cooking spray, and add two teaspoons of olive oil.
4. Sauté the mushrooms until they soften and change color.
5. Now lay one of your slabs of salmon fillet on a sheet pan you've coated with non-stick cooking spray or lined with non-stick foil. Lay the provolone on the salmon fillet. Drain the excess water off the tomatoes, and make a layer of them. Then top with the mushrooms.
6. Now lay the second piece of salmon on top.
7. Pierce with a few toothpicks or skewers to keep the layers together.
8. Use a basting brush to brush your salmon roast with the last teaspoon of olive oil. Sprinkle on the parsley. Now slide it into the oven for 20 to 30 minutes.
9. Slice in half through the layers to serve.

Nutrition: 352 Calories | Fat: 15g | Protein: 27g | Carbohydrates: 3g

Transcendent flounder

Prep Time: 10 minutes
Cook Time: 25 minutes
Servings: 4

Ingredients

- A quarter cup of butter
- Two pounds of flounder fillets in 4 servings
- Two lemons
- 1/3 cup of mayonnaise
- 1/3 cup of grated Parmesan cheese
- Four scallions

Directions

1. Turn on your broiler and arrange a rack about 4 inches (10 cm) deep.
2. Put the butter in a custard cup or glass measuring cup and microwave it for a minute to melt.
3. Lay a piece of foil over your broiler pan and coat it with non-stick cooking spray. Cup the edges a little. Now lay out the flounder fillets. Pour the batter evenly over the fillets and use a brush or the back of a spoon to make sure they're coated all over.
4. Halve the lemons, pick out the seeds, and squeeze the juice over the fish.
5. Slide the fish under the broiler. While it's cooking, mix together the mayonnaise and Parmesan.
6. By now, your fillets should be getting close to done; it doesn't take long. If they're cooking unevenly, turn the pan and let them cook for another minute.
7. When the flounder is getting opaque and flaky, spread the mayonnaise mixture evenly over them and slide them back under the broiler.
8. Slice up your scallions. Then check your fish—again, if the topping is browning unevenly, turn the pan to even it out and give it another minute or two.
9. When the topping is evenly golden, plate the fish, scatter the sliced scallion over each serving, and eat.

Nutrition: 481 Calories | Fat: 32g | Protein: 46g | Carbohydrates: 4g

Soup and Stew Recipes

California Soup

 Prep Time: 10 minutes   Cook Time: 0 minutes   Servings: 6

Directions

1. Pit and peel the avocado, and cut it into big chunks.
2. Purée in the blender with the broth (use caution when blending hot liquids) until very smooth, and serve.

Nutrition: 80 Calories | Fat: 6g | Protein: 4g | Carbohydrates: 3g

Ingredients

- One large or two small avocados, very ripe
- One quart of hot chicken broth

Sopa Tlalpeño

 Prep Time: 10 minutes   Cook Time: 30 minutes   Servings: 6

Directions

1. Pour the chicken broth into a large, heavy-bottomed saucepan, reserving a half cup of it, and place it over medium-high heat.
2. While it's heating, cut your chicken breast into thin strips or small cubes, then add to the broth. Let the whole thing simmer for 10 to 15 minutes or until the chicken is cooked through.
3. Put the reserved chicken broth in your blender with the chipotle and blend until the chipotle is puréed. Pour this mixture into the soup and stir.
4. Split the avocado in half, remove the seed, peel it, and cut it into Half-inch (1 cm) chunks. Add to the soup, along with the scallions, and salt and pepper to taste.
5. Ladle the soup into bowls and top each serving with shredded cheese.

Nutrition: 235 Calories | Fat: 13g | Protein: 26g | Carbohydrates: 4g

Ingredients

- One and a half quarts of chicken broth, divided
- One pound of boneless, skinless chicken breast
- One chipotle chile canned in adobo
- One Hass avocado
- Four scallions, sliced
- Salt and ground black pepper to taste
- 3/4 cup of shredded Monterey Jack cheese

Crab and Asparagus Soup

 Prep Time: 10 minutes    Cook Time: 15 minutes   Servings: 4

Directions

1. In a large, heavy saucepan, start the broth warming over medium heat. Stir in the ginger root.
2. Now snap the ends off of your asparagus where it wants to break naturally. Discard the ends, and slice the asparagus on the diagonal into half-inch (1 cm) pieces. When the soup is simmering, add the asparagus to it. Let it simmer for about 3 minutes.
3. While that's happening, beat the eggs until blended in a glass measuring cup. When the asparagus is just barely tender-crisp, take a fork in one hand and the cup of beaten eggs in the other.
4. Pour a stream of egg onto the surface of the soup, then stir with the fork. Repeat. It should take 3 or 4 additions to stir in all the eggs. Now you have lovely egg drops!
5. Stir in sherry, soy sauce, and sesame oil. Now add the crab, stir again, and cook for another 5 minutes or so before serving.

Nutrition: 237 Calories | Fat: 8g | Protein: 31g | Carbohydrates: 5g

Ingredients

- Two quarts of chicken broth
- Two teaspoons of grated fresh ginger root
- One pound of asparagus
- Two eggs
- One and a half tablespoons of dry sherry
- One tablespoon of soy sauce
- Two teaspoons of dark sesame oil
- Twelve ounces of lump crabmeat, fresh or canned

Cream of Mushroom Soup

 Prep Time: 10 minutes   Cook Time: 6 hours   Servings: 5

Directions

1. In a big, heavy skillet, sauté the mushrooms and onion in the butter until the mushrooms soften and change color.
2. Transfer them to your slow cooker. Add the broth. Cover the slow cooker, set it to low, and let it cook for 5 to 6 hours.
3. When the time's up, scoop out the vegetables with a slotted spoon and put them in your blender or food processor. Add enough broth to help them process easily and purée them finely.
4. Pour the puréed vegetables back into the slow cooker, scraping out every last bit with a rubber scraper.
5. Now stir in the heavy cream and sour cream and season with salt and pepper to taste. Thicken a bit with guar or xanthan if you think it needs it. Serve immediately

Nutrition: 217 Calories | Fat: 19g | Protein: 6g | Carbohydrates: 5g

Ingredients

- Eight ounces of mushrooms, sliced
- A quarter cup of chopped onion
- Two tablespoons of butter
- One quart of chicken broth
- Half cup of heavy cream
- Half cup of sour cream
- Salt and ground black pepper to taste
- Guar or xanthan (optional)

Cream of Salmon Soup

 Prep Time: 10 minutes  Cook Time: 35 minutes   Servings: 4

Directions

1. In a heavy saucepan, melt the butter over medium-low heat and add the onion and celery.
2. Sauté the vegetables for a few minutes until the onion starts turning translucent.
3. Meanwhile, pour the cream into a glass 2-cup (475 ml) measure or any other microwavable container similar in size to a pouring spout. Place it in the microwave and heat it at 50 percent power for 3 to 4 minutes.
4. Pour the cream into the saucepan and add the salmon and thyme. Break up the salmon as you stir the soup.
5. Heat until simmering, and serve.

Nutrition: 594 Calories | Fat: 54g | Protein: 23g | Carbohydrates: 5g

Ingredients

- One and a half tablespoons of butter
- A quarter cup of finely minced onion
- A quarter cup of finely minced celery
- Two cups of heavy cream
- One can (Fourteen ounces) of salmon, drained
- Half teaspoon of dried thyme

Creamy Broccoli Soup

Ingredients

- Two cups of low-Sodium vegetable broth
- Three cups of broccoli florets
- Eight ounces of silken tofu, undrained
- Three tablespoons of cornstarch
- Three tablespoons of nutritional yeast
- One teaspoon of onion powder
- One teaspoon of garlic powder
- A quarter teaspoon of black pepper
- 1/8 teaspoon of red pepper flakes

 Prep Time: 10 minutes   Cook Time: 8 minutes   Servings: 1

Directions

1. In a pot of vegetable broth, cook the broccoli florets and tofu until soft. Allow time for it to cool.
2. Pour the cool contents of the saucepan into a bowl and combine with an immersion blender until smooth. Alternatively, transfer the mixture of the pot to a big blender with caution.
3. Allow excessive steam to escape by removing the top stopper. Blend until it's completely smooth.
4. Mix one and a half cups of the soup with the cornstarch in a small basin. Whisk until the mixture is smooth.
5. Return the soup to the pot and stir in the cornstarch mixture before bringing it to a boil.
6. Combine the yeast and spices in a large mixing bowl. After that, serve.

Nutrition: 65 Calories | Fat: 1g | Protein: 4g | Carbohydrates: 9g

Egg Drop Soup

 Prep Time: 10 minutes   Cook Time: 15 minutes   Servings: 4

Directions

1. Put one cup or so of the chicken broth in your blender, turn it on low, and add the guar (if using).
2. Let it blend for a second, then put it in a large saucepan with the remaining three cups of broth. (If you're not using guar or xanthan, just put all the broth directly in a saucepan.)
3. Add the soy sauce, rice vinegar, ginger, and scallion. Over medium-high heat, bring to a simmer and cook for 5 minutes or so to let the flavors blend.
4. Beat your eggs in a glass measuring cup or small pitcher—something with a pouring lip.
5. Use a fork to stir the surface of the soup in a slow circle and pour in about one-quarter of the eggs, stirring as they cook and turning into shreds (which will happen almost instantaneously).
6. Repeat three more times, using up all the eggs. That's it.

Nutrition: 75 Calories | Fat: 4g | Protein: 8g | Carbohydrates: 2g

Ingredients

- One quart of chicken broth, divided
- A quarter teaspoon of guar or xanthan (optional)
- One tablespoon of soy sauce
- One tablespoon of rice vinegar
- Half teaspoon of grated fresh ginger root
- One scallion, sliced
- Two eggs

Not Pea Soup

 Prep Time: 10 minutes   Cook Time: 30 minutes   Servings: 5

Directions

1. In a heavy saucepan, melt the butter and start sautéing the onion, celery, and carrot over medium heat.
2. While that's happening, put your ham in your food processor with the S-blade in place, and pulse until it's chopped medium-fine. Scrape this out of the food processor and into the saucepan with the veggies. Give everything a stir while you're there.
3. Return the processor bowl to its base, and put the S-blade back in. Dump in the green beans, liquid and all, and run the processor until the beans are pureed quite smooth.
4. Go back and look at your sautéing vegetables; when they are soft, add the garlic.
5. Sauté it with the vegetables for just a minute.
6. Now dump in your green bean puree, and stir everything together. Add the thyme, bay leaves, and cayenne, and stir them in.
7. Turn the heat to low, and bring the soup to a simmer. Let it cook for 15 minutes or so.
8. Season with salt and pepper to taste, remove the bay leaves, and pour into mugs.

Nutrition: 120 Calories | Fat: 9g | Protein: 5g | Carbohydrates: 5g

Ingredients

- Three tablespoons of butter
- Half cup of chopped onion
- Half cup of chopped celery
- One medium carrot, grated
- Four ounces of ham
- Four cans (Fourteen and a half ounces, each) of green beans
- Half teaspoon of dried thyme
- Two bay leaves
- Two pinches of cayenne
- Salt and ground black pepper to taste

Old Fashioned Salmon Soup

Ingredients

- Two tablespoons of unsalted butter
- One medium chopped carrot
- Half cup of chopped celery
- Half cup of chopped onion
- One pound of sockeye salmon, cooked
- Two cups of reduced-sodium chicken broth
- Two cups of 1% low-fat milk
- 1/8 teaspoon of black pepper
- A quarter cup of cornstarch
- A quarter cup of water

 Prep Time: 10 minutes Cook Time: 30 minutes Servings: 8

Directions

1. Let the butter melt in a 3-quart saucepan on a stovetop burner. Add the vegetables to the saucepan and cook until tender.
2. Add the pre-cooked salmon chunks to the pan.
3. Stir together in the saucepan the chicken broth, milk, and black pepper. Bring mixture to a near-boil afterward, and reduce heat to simmer.
4. Combine the cornstarch and water and then slowly pour into the broth mixture, stirring, until the soup is thickened.
5. Simmer for another five minutes. Serve warm, and enjoy!

Nutrition: 155 Calories | Fat: 7g | Protein: 14g | Carbohydrates: 8g

Olive Soup

Ingredients

- One quart of chicken broth, divided
- Half teaspoon of guar or xanthan
- One cup of minced black olives (you can buy cans of minced black olives)
- One cup of heavy cream
- A quarter cup of dry sherry
- Salt or Vege-Sal and ground black pepper, to taste

 Prep Time: 10 minutes Cook Time: 20 minutes Servings: 6

Directions

1. Put half a cup of the chicken broth in the blender with the guar and blend for a few seconds.
2. Pour into a saucepan and add the remaining three and a half cups of broth and the olives.
3. Heat until simmering, then whisk in the cream. Bring back to a simmer, stir in the sherry, and season with salt and pepper to taste.

Nutrition: 189 Calories | Fat: 17g | Protein: 2g | Carbohydrates: 3g

Chinese-Style Tuna Soup

Ingredients

- One quart of chicken broth
- Two teaspoons of soy sauce
- One teaspoon of grated fresh ginger root
- Two eggs
- One can (Six ounces) of tuna packed in olive oil
- One and a half cups of chopped fresh spinach
- Two scallions, sliced thin

 Prep Time: 10 minutes Cook Time: 15 minutes Servings: 3

Directions

1. In a big saucepan, combine the chicken broth with the soy sauce and ginger. Put it over medium-high heat, and bring it to a boil, then turn the heat down till the broth is just simmering.
2. While the broth is heating, break the eggs into a little glass measuring cup or another container with a pouring lip. Beat them up with a fork.
3. When your soup is simmering, pour one-third of the egg into the soup, wait just 1 or 2 seconds, then stir with a fork, drawing out the egg into strands. Repeat with the rest of the egg in 2 or 3 more additions.
4. When you're done adding the egg, add the tuna and spinach. Heat through and serve with scallions on top.

Nutrition: 216 Calories | Fat: 9g | Protein: 27g | Carbohydrates: 3g

Roman Stew

Ingredients

- Two pounds of beef round, cut into 1-inch (2.5 cm) cubes
- One large onion, chopped
- Two cans (Six and a half ounces, each) of sliced mushrooms
- One and a half cups of beef broth
- Two teaspoons of Worcestershire sauce
- One teaspoon of beef bouillon concentrate
- One teaspoon of paprika
- Eight ounces of cream cheese
- Eight ounces of sour cream

 Prep Time: 10 minutes   Cook Time: 8 hours   Servings: 8

Directions

1. In your big, heavy skillet, over medium-high heat, brown the beef in the oil, working in a few batches. Transfer to a slow cooker.
2. Add the celery and garlic, then sprinkle the seasonings over everything. Now pour the canned tomatoes and the wine over everything. Cover the pot, set the slow cooker to low, and cook for 7 to 8 hours.
3. You can thicken the pot juices a little if you like, but it's not really necessary.

Nutrition: 413 Calories | Fat: 31g | Protein: 28g | Carbohydrates: 5g

Stracciatella

Ingredients

- One quart of chicken broth, divided
- Two eggs
- Half cup of grated Parmesan cheese
- Half a teaspoon of lemon juice
- Pinch of ground nutmeg
- Half teaspoon of dried marjoram

 Prep Time: 10 minutes   Cook Time: 20 minutes   Servings: 4

Directions

1. Put a quarter cup of the broth into a glass measuring cup or small pitcher. Pour the rest into a large saucepan over medium heat.
2. Add the eggs to the broth in the measuring cup and beat with a fork. Then add the Parmesan, lemon juice, and nutmeg, and beat with a fork until well blended.
3. When the broth in the saucepan is simmering, stir it with a fork as you add small amounts of the egg-and-cheese mixture until it's all stirred in. (Don't expect this to form long shreds like Chinese egg drop soup; because of the Parmesan, it makes small, fluffy particles instead.)
4. Add the marjoram, crushing it a bit between your fingers, and simmer the soup for another minute or so before serving.

Nutrition: 117 Calories | Fat: 7g | Protein: 12g | Carbohydrates: 2g

Tavern Soup

Ingredients

- One and a half quarts of chicken broth
- A quarter cup of finely diced celery
- A quarter cup of finely diced green bell pepper
- A quarter cup of shredded carrot
- A quarter cup of chopped fresh parsley
- Half teaspoon of ground black pepper
- One pound of sharp Cheddar cheese, shredded
- Twelve ounces of light beer
- Half teaspoon of salt or Vege-Sal
- A quarter teaspoon of hot pepper sauce
- Guar or xanthan, as needed

 Prep Time: 10 minutes  Cook Time: 8 hours   Servings: 8

Directions

1. Combine the broth, celery, green pepper, carrot, parsley, and black pepper in your slow cooker. Cover the pot, set the slow cooker to low, and let it cook for 6 to 8 hours.
2. When the time's up, either use a handheld blender to purée the vegetables right there in the slow cooker or scoop them out with a slotted spoon, purée them in your blender, and return them to the slow cooker.
3. Now whisk in the cheese a little at a time until it's all melted in. Add the beer, salt, and hot pepper sauce, and stir until the foaming stops.
4. Use guar as needed to thicken your soup until it's about the texture of heavy cream. Re-cover the pot, turn the slow cooker to high, and let it cook for another 20 minutes before serving.

Nutrition: 274 Calories | Fat: 20g | Protein: 18g | Carbohydrates: 3g

Salad Recipes

Asian Ginger Slaw

Prep Time: 10 minutes
Cook Time: 0 minutes
Servings: 8

Directions

1. Combine the cabbage, carrot, celery, and scallions in a salad bowl.
2. In a separate bowl, combine the mayonnaise, vinegar, ginger, soy sauce, and stevia.
3. Beat together until smooth, pour over the vegetables, toss, and serve.

Nutrition: 63 Calories | Fat: 6g | Protein: 1g | Carbohydrates: 3g

Ingredients

- Four cups of finely shredded napa cabbage
- A quarter cup of shredded carrot
- A quarter cup of thinly sliced celery— the pale, inner part of the rib bunch
- Two scallions, thinly sliced
- A quarter cup of mayonnaise
- Two tablespoons of rice vinegar
- One teaspoon of grated fresh ginger root
- One teaspoon of soy sauce
- Six drops of liquid stevia (plain)

Bacon, Tomato, and Cauliflower Salad

Ingredients

- Half head cauliflower
- Eight ounces of bacon, cooked until crisp and crumbled
- One large tomato, chopped
- Ten scallions, sliced, including all the crisp part of the green
- Half cup of mayonnaise
- Salt and ground black pepper to taste
- Lettuce (optional)

Prep Time: 10 minutes
Cook Time: 6 minutes
Servings: 6

Directions

1. Using the shredding disc of a food processor, shred the cauliflower. It can be steamed or microwaved till tender-crisp (about 5 minutes on high in a microwave).
2. In a large mixing dish, combine the cooked cauliflower, tomato, bacon, scallions, and mayonnaise.
3. Season with salt and pepper to taste.
4. Because this salad keeps its shape nicely when molded, you may pack it into a custard cup and unmold it onto a lettuce-lined dish if desired; it looks rather nice this way.

Nutrition: 374 Calories | Fat: 34g | Protein: 13g | Carbohydrates: 5g

Cheddar-Broccoli Salad

Prep Time: 10 minutes　　Cook Time: 10 minutes　　Servings: 8

Directions

1. In a large bowl, combine the broccoli, cheese, and onion. Combine the mayonnaise, Splenda, and vinegar; pour over the broccoli mixture and toss to coat. Refrigerate for at least 4 hours. Just before serving, stir in the bacon.
2. If you prefer, you can lightly steam the broccoli, then cool it before adding the other ingredients. But don't go beyond tender-crisp.

Nutrition: 455 Calories | Fat: 47g | Protein: 10g | Carbohydrates: 4g

Ingredients

- Six cups of fresh broccoli florets
- One and a half cups of shredded Cheddar cheese
- 1/3 cup of chopped onion
- One and a half cups of mayonnaise
- Half to 3/4 cup of Splenda
- Three tablespoons of red wine vinegar or cider vinegar
- Twelve slices of bacon, cooked and crumbled

Chicken Caesar Salad

Prep Time: 10 minutes　　Cook Time: 6 minutes　　Servings: 1

Directions

1. Grill chicken breast on an electric tabletop grill for about 5 minutes; you could sauté it if you prefer.
2. Meanwhile, assemble your lettuce, pour the dressing over it, and toss well. Pile it on your serving plate.
3. When the chicken breast is done, slice it into thin strips, and pile it on top of the lettuce.
4. Scatter the Parmesan over it, and dig in.

Nutrition: 402 Calories | Fat: 22g | Protein: 44g | Carbohydrates: 5g

Ingredients

- Six ounces of boneless, skinless chicken breast
- Three cups of torn romaine lettuce
- Two tablespoons of Caesar dressing, homemade or bottled
- Two tablespoons of Parmesan cheese

Chicken-Almond Noodle Salad

Prep Time: 10 minutes　　Cook Time: 10 minutes　　Servings: 2

Ingredients

- One package (Eight ounces) of tofu shirataki, fettuccine width
- Three tablespoons of slivered almonds
- One and a half teaspoons of coconut oil
- Two tablespoons of mayonnaise
- One tablespoon of almond butter
- Two teaspoons of soy sauce
- Half teaspoon of grated fresh ginger root
- Six drops Sriracha
- Half cup of cooked chicken
- Two scallions

Directions

1. Snip open the packet of tofu shirataki and pour it into a strainer in the sink. Rinse well, and use your kitchen shears to snip across them a couple of times, as they're so long.
2. Put the shirataki in a microwavable bowl, and nuke them on high for 2 minutes. Drain again, and repeat with another 2 minutes and another draining.
3. Let them cool while you do the rest.
4. In a small, heavy skillet over medium-low heat, start your almonds sautéing in your coconut oil.
5. Measure your mayonnaise, almond butter, soy sauce, ginger root, and Sriracha into a smallish dish, and stir together. This is your dressing.
6. Go back and stir your almonds! In fact, stir them once in between measuring the dressing ingredients. You don't want them to burn. When they're just getting golden, take them off the heat.
7. Cut your chicken into Half-inch (1 cm) cubes. Thinly slice your scallions, including the crisp part of the green.
8. For assembling the salad, dump the shirataki into a mixing bowl. Add the chicken, scallions, toasted almonds, and then the dressing. Stir it all up, and you're done!

Nutrition: 298 Calories | Fat: 26g | Protein: 15g | Carbohydrates: 5g

Chicken-Chili-Cheese Salad

Prep Time: 10 minutes　　Cook Time: 10 minutes　　Servings: 5

Ingredients

- Half head cauliflower
- One cup of diced celery
- Half red bell pepper, diced
- 1/3 cup of diced red onion
- A quarter cup of diced green chiles
- Two cups of diced cooked chicken
- Four ounces of Monterey Jack cheese, cut into 1/4-inch (6 mm) cubes
- 1/3 cup of mayonnaise
- One tablespoon of white vinegar
- One and a half teaspoons of lime juice
- One teaspoon of chili powder
- Half teaspoon of ground cumin
- Half a teaspoon of dried oregano
- Two ounces of sliced black olives, drained

Directions

1. First, chop your cauliflower into One and a half-inch (3.8 cm) chunks. Throw it in a microwavable casserole dish with a lid, add a couple of tablespoons (30 ml) of water, cover, and nuke it on high for 7 minutes.
2. While that's cooking, assemble your other vegetables, chicken, and cheese in a big mixing bowl.
3. As soon as the microwave beeps, pull out your cauliflower, uncover it, and drain it. Let it sit and cool for a few minutes.
4. You don't want it to melt your cheese. The cauliflower will cool faster if you stir it now and then.
5. While you're waiting for the cauliflower to cool, measure your mayonnaise, vinegar, lime juice, chili powder, cumin, and oregano. Stir it all together.
6. Dump it in with the chicken, cheese, and veggies, and stir everything around. Dump in the olives, pour on the dressing, and toss to coat. You can eat this right away, if you'd like, or chill it for a few hours.

Nutrition: 418 Calories | Fat: 34g | Protein: 23g | Carbohydrates: 5g

Chicken-Pecan Salad

Prep Time: 10 minutes
Cook Time: 0 minutes
Servings: 2

Directions

1. Toss all ingredients together, salting to taste. That's it!

   Nutrition: 640 Calories | Fat: 60g | Protein: 24g | Carbohydrates: 5g

Ingredients

- One and a half cups of diced leftover cooked chicken
- A quarter cup of chopped pecans
- 1/3 cup of mayonnaise
- Two big ribs celery, diced
- A quarter medium sweet red onion, diced
- Salt, to taste

Classic Spinach Salad

Prep Time: 10 minutes
Cook Time: 0 minutes
Servings: 3

Directions

1. Wash the spinach very well and dry. Tear up larger leaves. Combine with the onion in a salad bowl.
2. In a separate bowl, mix up the oil, vinegar, tomato paste, Stevia, grated red onion, mustard, and salt and pepper to taste.
3. Pour the mixture over the spinach and onion, and toss.
4. Top each serving with bacon and egg.

   Nutrition: 315 Calories | Fat: 29g | Protein: 11g | Carbohydrates: 4g

Ingredients

- Four cups of fresh spinach
- 1/8 large sweet red onion, thinly sliced
- Three tablespoons of (45 ml) oil—light olive oil or MCT oil
- Two tablespoons of (28 ml) cider vinegar
- Two teaspoons of tomato paste
- Nine drops of liquid stevia (plain)
- A small quarter onion, grated
- 1/8 teaspoon of dry mustard
- Salt and ground black pepper to taste
- Two slices of bacon, cooked until crisp and crumbled
- One hard-boiled egg, chopped

Club Sandwich Salad

 Prep Time: 10 minutes   Cook Time: 8 minutes   Servings: 6

Directions

1. Trim the leaves and the very bottom of the stem off your half head of cauliflower, whack it into chunks, and run it through the shredding blade of your food processor.
2. Put the resulting "cauli-rice" into a microwavable casserole dish with a lid, add a couple of tablespoons (30 ml) of water, and nuke on high for 6 minutes.
3. In the meantime, throw your turkey, lettuce, and tomato in a big salad bowl.
4. When your microwave beeps, pull out your cauli-rice and uncover it to stop the cooking. Let it cool for a few minutes so that it won't cook your lettuce and tomatoes! It will cool faster if you drain it and stir it now and then.
5. Measure and whisk together your mayonnaise, vinegar, lemon juice, and mustard.
6. Use your kitchen shears to snip the bacon into the salad, cutting it every 1/4 inch (6 mm) or so. Now add the cauli-rice, pour on the dressing, season with salt and pepper to taste, toss well, and serve.

Nutrition: 326 Calories | Fat: 26g | Protein: 21g | Carbohydrates: 5g

Ingredients

- Half head cauliflower
- Two cups of diced cooked turkey
- One heart romaine lettuce, cut crosswise in Half-inch (1 cm) strips—about Four cups of lettuce
- One large tomato, diced
- Half cup of mayonnaise
- Two tablespoons of cider vinegar
- Two tablespoons of lemon juice
- One teaspoon of spicy brown mustard
- Ten slices of bacon, cooked crisp
- Salt and ground black pepper to taste

Dilled Chicken Salad

 Prep Time: 10 minutes   Cook Time: 0 minutes   Servings: 2

Directions

1. Combine the chicken, celery, green pepper, and onion in a bowl.
2. In a separate bowl, mix together the mayonnaise, sour cream, and dill. Pour the mixture over the chicken and veggies, toss, add salt to taste, and serve.

Nutrition: 576 Calories | Fat: 48g | Protein: 33g | Carbohydrates: 5g

Ingredients

- One and a half cups of cooked chicken, diced
- One large rib celery, diced
- Half green bell pepper, diced
- A quarter medium sweet red onion, diced
- Three tablespoons of mayonnaise
- Three tablespoons of sour cream
- One teaspoon of dried dill weed
- Salt, to taste

Egg Salad

Prep Time: 10 minutes | Cook Time: 0 minutes | Servings: 2

Directions

1. Peel and coarsely chop your eggs, and cut up your veggies.
2. Assemble everything in a mixing bowl, then stir it up gently to preserve some hunks of yolk till everything is evenly distributed.
3. Season with salt and pepper to taste, and you're done.

Nutrition: 443 Calories | Fat: 43g | Protein: 14g | Carbohydrates: 5g

Ingredients

- Four hard-boiled eggs
- One rib of celery, diced
- Four scallions, sliced, including the crisp part of the green
- Five green olives, pitted and chopped
- 1/3 cup of mayonnaise
- Salt and ground black pepper to taste

Gorgonzola-and-Pesto Caesar Salad

Ingredients

- Six cups of torn romaine lettuce hearts
- Three tablespoons of extra-virgin olive oil
- One and a half tablespoons of pesto sauce
- 1/3 cup of crumbled Gorgonzola cheese

Prep Time: 10 minutes | Cook Time: 0 minutes | Servings: 4

Directions

1. Put your lettuce in a big salad bowl. Mix the olive oil and pesto together and then pour over the salad and stir well until it's all evenly coated.
2. Sprinkle the Gorgonzola over the whole thing, toss lightly again, and serve.

Nutrition: 64 Calories | Fat: 5g | Protein: 1g | Carbohydrates: 4g

Tuna Salad with Lemon and Capers

Ingredients

- One can (Five ounces) of tuna packed in olive oil
- Two ribs celery
- 1/3 cup of diced sweet red onion
- 1/3 cup of chopped fresh parsley
- One tablespoon of capers
- One tablespoon of lemon juice
- One tablespoon of mayonnaise

Prep Time: 10 minutes | Cook Time: 0 minutes | Servings: 2

Directions

1. Just drain your tuna lightly—you want some of the olive oil in the salad—and dice your celery.
2. Add to a mixing bowl with everything else, and combine lightly.

Nutrition: 212 Calories | Fat: 12g | Protein: 22g | Carbohydrates: 5g

Mixed Greens with Walnuts, Goat Cheese, and Raspberry Dressing

Ingredients

 Prep Time: 10 minutes
 Cook Time: 0 minutes
 Servings: 5

- Four cups of torn romaine lettuce
- Four cups of torn leaf lettuce
- Two cups of torn arugula
- Two cups of torn radicchio
- Two ounces of goat cheese
- Three tablespoons of chopped walnuts
- Half cup of Raspberry Vinaigrette
- A quarter cup of fresh raspberries

Directions

1. Assemble your lettuces, arugula, and radicchio in your salad bowl. Cut your goat cheese into little hunks.
2. Chop your walnuts and have them standing by.
3. Now pour your dressing over the greens, and toss.
4. Pile the salad onto five salad plates, and top each with a little goat cheese, some walnuts, and a few raspberries.

Nutrition: 229 Calories | Fat: 21g | Protein: 6g | Carbohydrates: 5g

Not-Quite-Middle-Eastern Salad

Ingredients

 Prep Time: 10 minutes
 Cook Time: 6 minutes
Servings: 6

- Half head cauliflower
- 2/3 cup of sliced stuffed olives (you can buy them pre-sliced in jars)
- Seven scallions, sliced
- Two cups of triple-washed fresh spinach, finely chopped
- One rib of celery, diced
- One small ripe tomato, finely diced
- A quarter cup of chopped fresh parsley
- A quarter cup of olive oil
- Two tablespoons of mayonnaise
- One tablespoon of red wine vinegar
- One teaspoon of minced garlic or Two cloves of garlic crushed
- Salt and ground black pepper to taste

Directions

1. Prepare the cauliflower for Cauli-Rice. Give it just 6 minutes of microwave steaming.
2. While that's cooking, prep the olives, scallions, spinach, celery, tomato, and parsley and combine them in a large salad bowl.
3. When the cauliflower comes out of the microwave, dump it into a strainer and run cold water over it for a moment or two to cool it. (You can let the cauliflower cool uncovered instead, but it will take longer.)
4. Drain the cauliflower well and dump it in with all the other vegetables. Add the oil, mayonnaise, vinegar, and garlic, and toss.
5. Add salt and pepper to taste, toss again, and serve.

Nutrition: 148 Calories | Fat: 15g | Protein: 1g | Carbohydrates: 5g

Sour Cream and Cuke Salad

Ingredients

 Prep Time: 10 minutes
 Cook Time: 0 minutes
 Servings: 10

- Two cucumbers, scrubbed but not peeled
- One green bell pepper
- Half large sweet red onion
- Half head cauliflower
- Two teaspoons of salt or Vege-Sal
- One cup of sour cream
- Two tablespoons of vinegar (cider vinegar is best, but wine vinegar will do)
- Two rounded teaspoons of dried dill weed

Directions

1. Slice the cucumbers, pepper, onion, and cauliflower as thinly as you possibly can.
2. Toss the vegetables well with the salt, and chill them in the refrigerator for an hour or two.
3. In a separate bowl, mix the sour cream, vinegar, and dill, combining well.
4. Remove the veggies from the fridge, drain off any water that has collected at the bottom of the bowl, and stir in the sour cream mixture.
5. Refrigerate for at least a few hours before serving.

Nutrition: 163 Calories | Fat: 16g | Protein: 4g | Carbohydrates: 2g

Sesame-Asparagus Salad

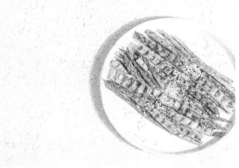

Prep Time: 10 minutes
Cook Time: 8 minutes
Servings: 4

Directions

1. Snap the ends off your asparagus where they want to break naturally. Cut the spears into One and a half-inch (3.5 cm) lengths, and put them in a microwave steamer or a microwavable casserole dish with a lid. Either way, add a couple of tablespoons of water (40 ml), cover, and microwave for just 3 to 4 minutes —you want it brilliantly green and just barely tender-crisp.
2. Uncover your asparagus as soon as the microwave beeps to stop the cooking. Drain well, and put in a deep, narrow bowl.
3. Combine the soy sauce and sesame oil. Pour over the asparagus, and toss. Chill for an hour or two.
4. When ready to serve, put the sesame seeds in a small, dry skillet over medium-low heat, and shake them until they start to "pop"—jump a bit—and smell toasty.
5. Remove from the heat. Stir the sesame seeds into the asparagus, and serve immediately.

Nutrition: 50 Calories | Fat: 4g | Protein: 2g | Carbohydrates: 4g

Ingredients

- One pound of asparagus
- Four teaspoons of soy sauce
- Two teaspoons of dark sesame oil
- One tablespoon of sesame seeds

Shrimp Caesar Salad

Prep Time: 10 minutes
Cook Time: 8 minutes
Servings: 1

Directions

1. Assemble your lettuce, pour the dressing over it, and toss well. Pile it on your serving plate.
2. Slice the shrimp into thin strips, and pile them on top of the lettuce.
3. Scatter the Parmesan over it, and dig in.

Nutrition: 317 Calories | Fat: 19g | Protein: 30g | Carbohydrates: 5g

Ingredients

- Ten to twelve good-size precooked shrimp
- Three cups of torn romaine lettuce
- Two tablespoons of Caesar dressing, homemade or bottled
- Two tablespoons of Parmesan cheese

Sirloin Salad

 Prep Time: 10 minutes   Cook Time: 15 minutes   Servings: 1

Directions

1. Preheat your grill or broiler and cook the steak to your liking.
2. Meanwhile, toss the lettuce with the vinaigrette and arrange it on a plate.
3. When your steak is done, slice it medium-thin across the grain, and arrange it on the bed of lettuce.
4. Scatter the onion and cheese over it, arrange the tomato wedges around it, and it's done.

Nutrition: 496 Calories | Fat: 36g | Protein: 36g | Carbohydrates: 5g

Ingredients

- Six ounces of sirloin steak, 1 inch (2.5 cm) thick
- One cup of torn romaine lettuce
- One tablespoon of vinaigrette—French Vinaigrette or Italian Vinaigrette would be good
- Two tablespoons of minced red onion
- Two tablespoons of crumbled blue cheese
- A large quarter tomato, cut into wedges

Unpotato Salad

 Prep Time: 10 minutes   Cook Time: 8 minutes   Servings: 1-2

Directions

1. Put the cauliflower in a microwavable casserole dish, add just a tablespoon (15 ml) or so of water, and cover. Cook it on high for 7 minutes, and let it sit, covered, for another 3 to 5 minutes. You want your cauliflower tender but not mushy.
2. Use the time while the cauliflower cooks to dice your celery and onion.
3. Drain the cooked cauliflower and combine it with the celery and onion in a really big bowl.
4. In a separate bowl, combine the mayonnaise, vinegar, salt, pepper, and stevia. Pour the mixture over the vegetables and mix well.
5. Mix in the chopped eggs last, and only stir lightly to preserve some small hunks of yolk. Chill and serve.

Nutrition: 298 Calories | Fat: 33g | Protein: 3g | Carbohydrates: 2g

Ingredients

- One large head of cauliflower, cut into small chunks
- Two cups of diced celery
- One cup of diced red onion
- Two cups of mayonnaise
- A quarter cup of cider vinegar
- Two teaspoons of salt or Vege-Sal
- Half teaspoon of ground black pepper
- Twelve drops of liquid stevia (plain)
- Four hard-boiled eggs, chopped

Southwestern Potato Salad

Prep Time: 10 minutes
Cook Time: 8 minutes
Servings: 6

Directions

1. First, cut your cauliflower into Half-inch (1 cm) chunks—don't bother coring it first; just trim the bottom of the stem and cut up the core with the rest of it.
2. Put your cauliflower chunks in a microwavable casserole dish with a lid, add a few tablespoons of water, and cook it on high for 7 minutes.
3. When your cauliflower is done, drain it and put it in a large mixing bowl. In a medium bowl, whisk together the mayonnaise, mustard, and lime juice; then, pour it over the cauliflower and mix well.
4. Cut the jalapeño in half, remove the seeds, and mince it fine. Add it to the salad along with the cilantro, onion, and garlic; mix again.
5. Finally, cut the stem out of the tomato and cut the tomato into smallish dice, then carefully stir it in.
6. Chill the salad for a few hours before serving.

Nutrition: 158 Calories | Fat: 16g | Protein: 2g | Carbohydrates: 5g

Ingredients

- Half head cauliflower
- Half cup of mayonnaise
- Two tablespoons of spicy mustard
- One tablespoon of lime juice
- One small jalapeño
- 1/3 cup of chopped fresh cilantro
- 1/3 cup of diced red onion
- One clove of garlic, crushed
- One small tomato

Spinach-Plum Salad

Prep Time: 10 minutes
Cook Time: 0 minutes
Servings: 8

Directions

1. Dump your baby spinach in your big salad bowl.
2. Halve the plums, remove the pits, and cut into Half-inch (1 cm) dice. Slice your scallions, including the crisp part of the green.
3. In a small bowl, whisk together the peanut oil, rice vinegar, soy sauce, ginger, and stevia.
4. Pour this over the spinach and toss it till it's coated with the dressing.
5. Pile the spinach on eight salad plates, top each serving with plum cubes and scallions, and serve.

Nutrition: 51 Calories | Fat: 4g | Protein: 2g | Carbohydrates: 4g

Ingredients

- Twelve cups of baby spinach
- Two red plums
- Two scallions, sliced
- Two tablespoons of peanut oil, light olive oil, or MCT oil
- Two tablespoons of rice vinegar
- One teaspoon of soy sauce
- Half teaspoon of grated fresh ginger root
- Three drops of liquid stevia (plain)

Toasted Salad

Prep Time: 10 minutes
Cook Time: 0 minutes
Servings: 8

Directions

1. Crush the clove of garlic in a small bowl, cover it with olive oil, and set it aside.
2. Wash and dry your romaine, break it up into a bowl, and add the parsley, pepper, cucumber, and onion.
3. Pour the garlic-flavored oil over the salad and toss until every leaf is covered.
4. Sprinkle on the lemon juice to taste and toss again. Then sprinkle on the Worcestershire sauce as desired and toss again.
5. Finally, sprinkle on the Parmesan and toss one last time. Top with the tomato wedges, and serve.

Nutrition: 156 Calories | Fat: 14g | Protein: 3g | Carbohydrates: 5g

Ingredients

- One clove of garlic
- Half cup of extra-virgin olive oil
- One head of romaine lettuce
- Half cup of chopped fresh parsley
- Half green bell pepper, diced
- A quarter cucumber, quartered and sliced
- A quarter sweet red onion, sliced paper-thin
- Three tablespoons of lemon juice
- Three teaspoons of Worcestershire sauce
- A quarter cup of grated Parmesan cheese
- One medium ripe tomato, cut into thin wedges

Tuna Salad

Prep Time: 10 minutes
Cook Time: 0 minutes
Servings: 2

Directions

1. Dice up the vegetable.
2. Then add the tuna, mayonnaise, and pickles, and mix it up

Nutrition: 424 Calories | Fat: 37g | Protein: 22g | Carbohydrates: 5g

Ingredients

- Two big ribs of celery or three smaller ones
- Half green bell pepper
- A quarter medium sweet red onion
- One can (five ounces) of tuna packed in olive oil
- 1/3 cup of mayonnaise
- Two tablespoons of minced sugar-free bread-and-butter pickles

Vegetable and Side Recipes

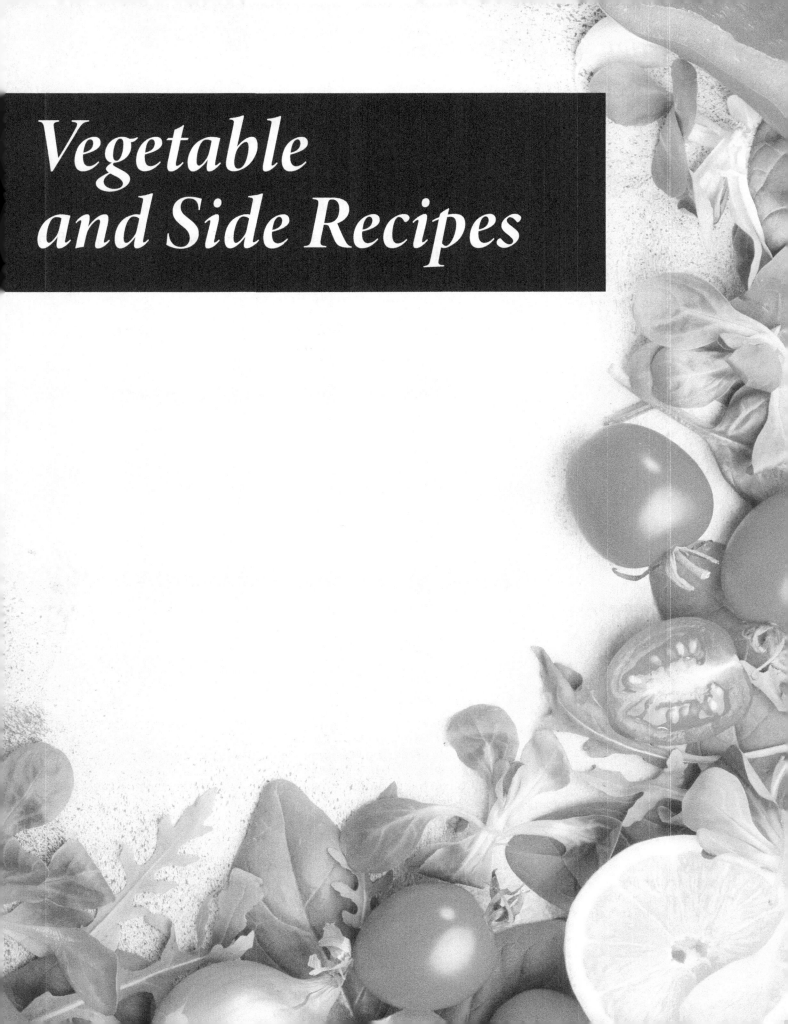

Asparagus with Mushrooms and Hazelnuts

Ingredients

- 1/8 teaspoon of sea salt
- Half pound of fresh asparagus ends trimmed
- Two cups of mushrooms
- One tablespoon of hazelnuts, toasted and finely chopped
- One tablespoon of lemon juice
- Ground black pepper to taste
- One tablespoon of coconut oil
- A quarter cup of green onions, sliced

 Prep Time: 10 minutes  Cook Time: 15 minutes   Servings: 4

Directions

1. In a small bowl, combine a half tablespoon of oil, lemon juice, salt, and pepper.
2. In a saucepan, bring water to a boil, and then add the asparagus. Bring to a boil for a few minutes. In a pan over high heat, heat the remaining half tablespoon of oil.
3. Cook the mushrooms until they are softened. Add the green onions and cook for another minute. Cook for another 3 minutes after adding the asparagus.
4. Remove the pan from the heat and drizzle in the lemon juice mixture slowly.
5. Sprinkle the toasted hazelnuts over the top.

Nutrition: 66 Calories | Fat: 1g | Protein: 3g | Carbohydrates: 7g

Cucumber-Wrapped Vegetable Rolls

Ingredients

- Half cup of finely shredded red cabbage
- Half cup of grated carrot
- A quarter cup of julienned red bell pepper
- A quarter cup of julienned scallion, both green and white parts
- A quarter cup of chopped cilantro
- One tablespoon of olive oil
- A quarter teaspoon of ground cumin
- A quarter teaspoon of freshly ground black pepper
- One English cucumber, sliced into eight very thin strips with a vegetable peeler

 Prep Time: 10 minutes   Cook Time: 30 minutes   Servings: 8

Directions

1. In a medium-sized bowl, toss together the cabbage, carrot, red pepper, scallion, cilantro, olive oil, cumin, and black pepper until well mixed.
2. Evenly divide the vegetable filling among the cucumber strips, placing the filling close to one end of the strip.
3. Roll up the cucumber strips around the filling and secure them with a wooden pick.
4. Repeat with each cucumber strip.

Nutrition: 28 Calories | Fat: 2g | Protein: 0g | Carbohydrates: 4g

Cauli-Rice

Prep Time: 10 minutes | Cook Time: 8 minutes | Servings: 4

Directions

1. Trim the leaves and the very bottom of the stem from your cauliflower. Cut it into chunks, and run them through the shredding blade of your food processor.
2. Steam lightly—add a little water and steam for 6 to 7 minutes on high in the microwave.

Nutrition: 18 Calories | Fat: 0g | Protein: 1g | Carbohydrates: 4g

Ingredients

- Half head cauliflower

Chard and Cashew Sauté

Ingredients

- One bunch of Swiss chard
- Half cup of cashews
- One tablespoon of coconut oil
- Sea salt (optional)
- Ground black pepper

Prep Time: 10 minutes | Cook Time: 10 minutes | Servings: 2

Directions

1. Remove the rough stems from the Swiss chard and wash them.
2. Heat a skillet over medium heat and pour in the oil once it is heated.
3. Swiss chard should be thinly sliced.
4. Add the Swiss chard and cashews to the heated skillet. Only 1 minute of sautéing is required.
5. Serve warm, seasoning with sea salt and ground black pepper to taste.

Nutrition: 57 Calories | Fat: 3g | Protein: 1g | Carbohydrates: 6g

Cauliflower Purée

Prep Time: 10 minutes | Cook Time: 15 minutes | Servings: 6

Directions

1. Trim the very bottom of the cauliflower stem, and remove the leaves. Cut the rest into chunks.
2. Put the cauliflower in a microwavable casserole dish with a lid, or a microwave steamer, add a couple of tablespoons of water, and cover.
3. Microwave it on high for 12 minutes, or until quite tender but not sulfury smelling. Drain it thoroughly.
4. Now puree it in your food processor.
5. Work in the cream cheese and butter, then season with salt and pepper to taste.

Nutrition: 125 Calories | Fat: 11g | Protein: 3g | Carbohydrates: 5g

Ingredients

- One head cauliflower
- Two ounces of cream cheese
- A quarter cup of butter
- Salt and ground black pepper to taste

Roasted Asparagus

 Prep Time: 10 minutes   Cook Time: 12 minutes   Servings: 10

Directions

1. Preheat the oven to 450°F.
2. Gently bend each asparagus stalk until it snaps or breaks. Toss the part that was below the break.
3. Pour the olive oil into an ovenproof dish or shallow baking pan large enough to accommodate the asparagus.
4. Add salt and pepper—freshly ground is best—to taste.
5. Place the asparagus in the olive oil and roll it in the oil and seasonings until it is well coated.
6. Place in the preheated oven and roast until just tender—5 to 7 minutes for thin spears, 8 to 10 for medium, 10 to 12 for thick.
7. Remove and serve immediately.

Nutrition: 29 Calories | Fat: 1g | Protein: 2g | Carbohydrates: 3g

Ingredients

- Three pounds of asparagus, all about the same thickness
- One tablespoon of olive oil
- Salt and ground black pepper to taste

Roasted Cauliflower with Tahini Sauce

 Prep Time: 10 minutes   Cook Time: 45 minutes   Servings: 4

Directions

1. Heat oven to 450°F.
2. Place cauliflower florets in a large roasting pan.
3. Roast vegetables until tender, occasionally stirring, for about 35 minutes.
4. Meanwhile, combine tahini, lemon juice, garlic, and A quarter cup of water in a bowl and season with salt.
5. Serve cauliflower hot or at room temperature with tahini sauce.

Nutrition: 58 Calories | Fat: 5g | Protein: 4g | Carbohydrates: 9g

Ingredients

- Two tablespoons of extra-virgin olive oil or avocado oil
- One teaspoon of ground cumin
- One smaller cauliflower head, cored and cut into 1 1/2" florets
- Salt and ground black pepper
- A quarter cup of tahini
- Two cloves of garlic smashed and minced into a paste
- Juice of a quarter lemon

Roasted Curried Cauliflower

 Prep Time: 10 minutes
 Cook Time: 40 minutes
 Servings: 4

Directions

1. Preheat the oven to 450 degrees Fahrenheit.
2. In a large roasting pan, place cauliflower florets.
3. Toss the cauliflower with the onions. In a skillet over medium heat, dry roast coriander and cumin seeds until lightly browned about 5 minutes. Crush with a pestle in a mortar.
4. Fill a basin halfway with seeds. Combine the curry paste, lemon juice, oil, paprika, and salt in a mixing bowl.
5. Toss the vegetables in the dressing to coat them. Sprinkle pepper over the vegetables and spread them out in a single layer.
6. Cook, occasionally stirring, until veggies are tender, about 35 minutes.
7. Garnish with cilantro and serve immediately.

Nutrition: 38 Calories | Fat: 1g | Protein: 1g | Carbohydrates: 7g

Ingredients

- Two cups of cauliflower florets
- Half chopped small onion
- A quarter teaspoon of coriander seeds
- A quarter teaspoon of cumin seeds
- Two tablespoons of olive oil or cumin oil
- A quarter cup of lemon juice
- One teaspoon of curry paste
- A quarter teaspoon of hot paprika
- A quarter teaspoon of salt
- Two tablespoons of chopped cilantro

Sautéed Collard Greens

 Prep Time: 10 minutes
 Cook Time: 25 minutes
 Servings: 6

Directions

1. Blanch the collard greens by putting them into a pot of boiling water for 30 seconds.
2. Strain the water and transfer the greens to a large bowl of ice water. Let it cool, then strain and dry the greens.
3. In a large pan on medium-high heat, melt the butter and oil together.
4. Add onions and garlic, and cook until slightly browned, about 4–6 minutes. Add the blanched collard greens and black and red pepper, then cook for 5–8 minutes on high heat, stirring constantly.
5. Remove from heat, add vinegar, if desired, and stir.

Nutrition: 110 Calories | Fat: 3g | Protein: 2g | Carbohydrates: 5g

Ingredients

- Eight cups of chopped and blanched fresh collard greens
- Two tablespoons of olive oil
- One tablespoon of butter, unsalted
- A quarter cup of onions, finely diced
- One tablespoon of fresh garlic, chopped
- One teaspoon of crushed red pepper flakes
- One teaspoon of ground black pepper
- One tablespoon of vinegar

Stir-Fry Vegetables

 Prep Time: 10 minutes **Cook Time:** 30 minutes **Servings:** 4

Ingredients

- A quarter cup of canola oil
- Three and a half cups of green pepper
- Three and a half cups of red pepper
- One and a half cups of fresh sliced mushrooms
- One cup of celery
- A quarter cup of onion
- One garlic clove
- Half teaspoon sugar
- Half teaspoon dried oregano
- A quarter teaspoon of salt
- A quarter teaspoon of pepper
- One teaspoon of wine vinegar
- Half green hard-ripe tomato
- One cup of canned sliced water chestnuts

Directions

1. Green and red peppers, cut Celery should be sliced, and onion should be chopped. Crush the garlic cloves.
2. In a large skillet, heat the oil, then add the red pepper, green pepper, mushrooms, onion, celery, garlic, oregano, sugar, salt, and pepper to taste.
3. Over medium-high heat, stir-fry the vegetables.
4. Combine the tomato, vinegar, and drained water chestnuts in a mixing bowl. Cook until completely heated.

Nutrition: 84 Calories | Fat: 6g | Protein: 1g | Carbohydrates: 9g

Sauces, Dips and Dressing Recipes

Aioli

Prep Time: 10 minutes Cook Time: 0 minutes Servings: 12 or One and a half cups

Ingredients

- Three cloves of garlic
- Half teaspoon of salt
- Two egg yolks
- One cup of virgin olive oil or MCT oil

Directions

1. Put your garlic cloves and salt in your food processor, and run till the garlic is pulverized.
2. Add the egg yolks, and run till everything is well blended. While that's happening, you can measure your oil into a measuring cup with a pouring lip.
3. Now with the processor running, pour in the oil in a very thin stream, about the diameter of a pencil lead. When it's all in, it's done! Store in a lidded jar in the fridge.

Nutrition: 172 Calories | Fat: 19g | Protein: 1g | Carbohydrates: 0.2g

Bacon Butter

Prep Time: 10 minutes Cook Time: 6 minutes Servings: 4

Ingredients

- Four slices of bacon
- Half cup of butter
- One teaspoon of spicy brown or Dijon mustard

Directions

1. Lay your bacon on a microwave bacon rack or on a glass pie plate.
2. Microwave on high for 4 to 5 minutes or until crisp.
3. In the meantime, throw your butter in your food processor and add the mustard. Pulse until well combined.
4. By now, your bacon is done. Pull it out of the microwave and use your kitchen shears to snip it into the food processor in little bits. Pulse the food processor to mix in the bacon.

Nutrition: 120 Calories | Fat: 13g | Protein: 1g | Carbohydrates: 0.3g

Blue Cheese Steak Butter

Prep Time: 10 minutes Cook Time: 0 minutes Servings: 8

Ingredients

- Eight ounces of blue cheese, crumbled
- 3/4 cup of softened butter
- Two cloves of garlic, crushed
- One tablespoon of spicy brown mustard
- Three drops of Tabasco sauce

Directions

1. Just plunk all this stuff in your food processor and run it until it's well blended and smooth. Put it in a pretty dish and chill it.
2. Then drop a good, rounded tablespoonful over each serving of freshly grilled or broiled steak.

Nutrition: 255 Calories | Fat: 26g | Protein: 6g | Carbohydrates: 1g

Cheese Sauce

 Prep Time: 10 minutes

 Cook Time: 20 minutes

 Servings: 4 or one cup

Directions

1. In a saucepan over the lowest heat, heat the cream and cream cheese together, whisking until they're combined.
2. Whisk in the Cheddar a little at a time, letting each addition melt before adding more.
3. Whisk in the horseradish mustard, if using, and you're done.

Nutrition: 316 Calories | Fat: 30g | Protein: 10g | Carbohydrates: 2g

Ingredients

- 2/3 cup of heavy cream
- A quarter cup of whipped cream cheese
- Five ounces of Cheddar cheese, shredded
- One teaspoon of horseradish mustard (optional)

Chili-Cocoa Rub

Ingredients

- A quarter cup of salt or Vege-Sal
- Three tablespoons of ground cumin
- Three tablespoons of garlic powder
- Two tablespoons of ground black pepper
- Two tablespoons of chili powder
- Two tablespoons of Splenda or Stevia in the Raw
- One tablespoon of erythritol
- One tablespoon of onion powder
- Two teaspoons of cocoa powder

 Prep Time: 10 minutes

 Cook Time: 0 minutes

 Servings: 16 or One cup

Directions

1. Stir everything together and store in a clean, used spice shaker.
2. Use on steaks, pork chops, burgers, and ribs. It's so good!

Nutrition: 17 Calories | Fat: 0.2g | Protein: 1g | Carbohydrates: 3g

Chipotle Mayonnaise

 Prep Time: 10 minutes
 Cook Time: 0 minutes
 Servings: 16 or One cup

Directions

1. Put everything in your food processor, and run till the chipotle and garlic are pulverized. That's it.

Nutrition: 99 Calories | Fat: 12g | Protein: 0.2g | Carbohydrates: 0.1g

Ingredients
- One cup of mayonnaise
- One chipotle chile canned in adobo
- Half teaspoon of ground cumin
- One clove of garlic

Cinnamon Sugar

 Prep Time: 5 minutes
 Cook Time: 10 minutes
 Servings: 10 or 1/3 cup

Directions

1. Stir the two together. That's it.

Nutrition: 4 Calories | Fat: 0.1g | Protein: 0.1g | Carbohydrates: 1g

Ingredients
- A quarter cup of Splenda, Stevia in the Raw, or erythritol
- One tablespoon of ground cinnamon

Cocktail Sauce

 Prep Time: 10 minutes
 Cook Time: 0 minutes
 Servings: 6 or Half cup

Directions

1. Just mix everything together. Done!

Nutrition: 2 Calories | Fat: 0.1g | Protein: 0.1g | Carbohydrates: 1g

Ingredients
- 1/3 cup of Heinz Reduced Sugar Ketchup
- One tablespoon of Tabasco sauce
- One tablespoon of lemon juice
- One tablespoon of prepared horseradish

Classic Rub

 Prep Time: 10 minutes  Cook Time: 8 minutes   Servings: 13 or ¾ cup

Directions

1. Just stir everything together. Store in a clean old spice shaker.

   Nutrition: 15 Calories | Fat: 0.3g | Protein: 1g | Carbohydrates: 3g

Ingredients

- A quarter cup of erythritol
- Two tablespoons of paprika
- One tablespoon of celery salt
- One tablespoon of chili powder
- One tablespoon of garlic powder
- One tablespoon of onion powder
- One tablespoon of seasoned salt
- Two teaspoons of black pepper
- One teaspoon of lemon pepper
- One teaspoon of dry mustard
- One teaspoon of dried sage
- Half a teaspoon of cayenne
- Half teaspoon of dried thyme

Coleslaw Dressing

 Prep Time: 10 minutes   Cook Time: 8 minutes   Servings: 8 or One cup

Directions

1. Combine all the ingredients well and toss with coleslaw mix.

   Nutrition: 132 Calories | Fat: 15g | Protein: 1g | Carbohydrates: 1g

Ingredients

- Half cup of mayonnaise
- Half cup of sour cream
- One and a half tablespoons of cider vinegar
- One and a half teaspoons of prepared mustard
- Half to One teaspoon of salt or Vege-Sal
- Twelve drops of liquid stevia (plain)

Easy Alfredo Sauce

Ingredients

- Half cup of chive-and-onion cream cheese
- Two tablespoons of heavy cream
- One tablespoon of butter
- One clove of garlic, crushed
- Two tablespoons of grated Parmesan cheese

 Prep Time: 10 minutes Cook Time: 10 minutes Servings: 4 or ¾ cup

Directions

1. In a small saucepan over low heat, combine the chive cream cheese, heavy cream, butter, and garlic.
2. Whisk until you have a smooth sauce. Whisk in the Parmesan, and you're done.

Nutrition: 134 Calories | Fat: 13g | Protein: 2g | Carbohydrates: 1g

French Vinaigrette

Ingredients

- 3/4 cup of extra-virgin olive oil
- 1/3 cup of wine vinegar
- One teaspoon of Dijon mustard
- One clove of garlic, crushed
- Half teaspoon of salt
- A quarter teaspoon of ground black pepper

 Prep Time: 10 minutes Cook Time: 8 minutes Servings: 12

Directions

1. Just put everything in a clean jar, lid it tightly, and shake vigorously. You can store it in the jar and just shake it up again before use.

Nutrition: 121 Calories | Fat: 14g | Protein: 0.3g | Carbohydrates: 1g

Italian Vinaigrette

Ingredients

- 2/3 cup of extra-virgin olive oil
- 1/3 cup of wine vinegar
- Half teaspoon of salt
- Half a teaspoon of dried oregano
- A quarter teaspoon of dried basil
- A quarter teaspoon of ground black pepper
- One tiny pinch of red pepper flakes
- Two cloves of garlic, crushed

 Prep Time: 10 minutes Cook Time: 8 minutes Servings: 1

Directions

1. Assemble everything in a jar, lid it tightly, and shake-shake-shake.
2. Store it in the jar in the fridge, and just shake it again before using.

Nutrition: 108 Calories | Fat: 12g | Protein: 0.1g | Carbohydrates: 1g

Gorgonzola Sauce

 Prep Time: 10 minutes Cook Time: 10 minutes Servings: 4

Directions

1. In a heavy saucepan, melt the butter over medium-low heat and start sautéing the minced shallot.
2. When it's soft, add the half-and-half and the crumbled Gorgonzola. Turn the heat down to low and cook, often stirring, until the Gorgonzola is melted

Nutrition: 186 Calories | Fat: 16g | Protein: 7g | Carbohydrates: 3g

Ingredients

- One tablespoon of butter
- One shallot, minced
- 3/4 cup of half-and-half
- One cup of crumbled Gorgonzola cheese

Maple Butter

Ingredients

- Half cup of butter softened
- 1/8 teaspoon of maple extract
- Twenty drops of liquid stevia (English toffee)

 Prep Time: 10 minutes Cook Time: 8 minutes Servings: 18 or Half cups

Directions

1. Just run everything through the food processor till it's combined. Store in an airtight container in the fridge.

Nutrition: 102 Calories | Fat: 11g | Protein: 0.1g | Carbohydrates: 0.1g

Maple-Chipotle Glaze

 Prep Time: 10 minutes Cook Time: 0 minutes Servings: 5 or a quarter cup

Directions

1. Put everything in your food processor, and run it till the chipotle's minced fine.

Nutrition: 2 Calories | Fat: 0g | Protein: 0.1g | Carbohydrates: 0.2g

Ingredients

- Three tablespoons of erythritol
- One tablespoon of water
- One chipotle chile canned in adobo
- One clove of garlic, crushed
- Six drops of liquid stevia (English toffee)
- Six drops of maple extract

Raspberry Vinaigrette

Ingredients

- Half shallot
- Half teaspoon of Dijon mustard
- A quarter cup of raspberry vinegar—read the labels to find one with no sugar
- Six drops of liquid stevia (plain)
- Half cup of olive oil
- Salt and ground black pepper to taste

Prep Time: 10 minutes | Cook Time: 8 minutes | Servings: 8 or ¾ cup

Directions

1. Put the shallot and mustard in your food processor, and turn it on. As the shallots are reaching the minced stage, add the raspberry vinegar and liquid stevia. Now slowly pour in the olive oil. When it's well incorporated, turn off the processor.
2. Taste, add salt and pepper, then pulse just another second or two to mix, and it's ready to use.

Nutrition: 121 Calories | Fat: 14g | Protein: 0.1g | Carbohydrates: 1g

Sun-Dried Tomato and Basil Mayonnaise

Prep Time: 10 minutes | Cook Time: 8 minutes | Servings: 1

Directions

1. Put everything in your food processor with the S-blade in place.
2. Now run the processor, stopping it every now and then to scrape down the sides with a rubber scraper to get things back into the path of the blade.

Nutrition: 68 Calories | Fat: 8g | Protein: 0.1g | Carbohydrates: 1g

Ingredients

- Half cup of mayonnaise
- Two packed tablespoons of chopped sun-dried tomatoes
- Two packed tablespoons of chopped fresh basil
- One tablespoon of lemon juice
- One teaspoon of water
- One clove of garlic, minced

Tangy Honey Mustard Dressing

 Prep Time: 10 minutes   Cook Time: 0 minutes   Servings: 12 or one cup

Directions

1. Just assemble everything in a clean jar, lid it tightly, and shake like mad. Store in the fridge, right in the jar, and shake again before using.

   Nutrition: 6 Calories | Fat: 0.1g | Protein: 0.1g | Carbohydrates: 1g

Ingredients

- Half cup of light olive oil
- A quarter cup of cider vinegar
- A quarter cup of brown mustard
- 1/8 teaspoon of liquid stevia (plain)
- A quarter teaspoon of ground black pepper
- A quarter teaspoon of salt

Wasabi Mayonnaise

 Prep Time: 10 minutes   Cook Time: 0 minutes   Servings: 8 or Half cup

Directions

1. Just combine everything in a bowl, and whisk together well. Unbelievably good.

   Nutrition: 100 Calories | Fat: 12g | Protein: 1g | Carbohydrates: 1g

Ingredients

- Half cup of mayonnaise
- Two teaspoons of soy sauce
- One teaspoon of lemon juice
- One teaspoon of wasabi paste
- Three drops of liquid stevia

Dessert Recipes

Brownies

Prep Time: 10 minutes   Cook Time: 25 minutes   Servings: 12

Directions

1. Preheat the oven to 350°F.
2. Coat an 8-inch (20 cm) square baking pan with non-stick cooking spray.
3. In the top of a double boiler or in a saucepan over a heat diffuser, set on the lowest possible heat, and melt the chocolate and butter together. Stir until they're well combined. Scrape this into a mixing bowl.
4. Add the erythritol, stir well, then stir in the Splenda. Next, beat in the eggs, one at a time. Stir in the protein powder and salt.
5. Pour into the prepared pan and bake for 15 to 20 minutes. Do not overbake! Cut into 12 squares, and let cool in the pan.
6. Store in an airtight container in the refrigerator.

Nutrition: 208 Calories | Fat: 19g | Protein: 9g | Carbohydrates: 2g

Ingredients

- Two ounces of unsweetened baking chocolate
- One cup of butter
- Half cup of erythritol
- Half cup of Splenda
- Two eggs
- Half cup of vanilla whey protein powder
- Pinch of salt

Cheesecake

Prep Time: 10 minutes   Cook Time: 15 minutes   Servings: 10

Directions

1. Preheat the oven to 375°F.
2. Mix everything together thoroughly with an electric mixer. Spread in a buttered 9-inch (23 cm) springform pan.
3. Bake the cheesecake for 10 minutes. Reduce the heat to 250°F (120°C) and bake for an additional hour.
4. At the end of the hour, remove the cake and run a knife around the edge of the pan.
5. Return the cake to the warm oven and let it sit until the oven cools (approximately another hour).
6. Chill in the fridge overnight and enjoy!

Nutrition: 365 Calories | Fat: 36g | Protein: 10g | Carbohydrates: 3g

Ingredients

- Two pounds of cream cheese at room temperature
- Two cups of Splenda
- Three tablespoons of heavy cream
- Five eggs

Cinnamon Nuts

 Prep Time: 10 minutes Cook Time: 8 minutes Servings: 4

Ingredients

- Two tablespoons of butter
- One cup of shelled walnuts, pecans, or a combination of the two (I like the combo)
- Two tablespoons of erythritol
- Half teaspoon of ground cinnamon

Directions

1. Melt the butter in a heavy skillet over medium heat, then add the nuts. Cook for 5 to 6 minutes, stirring from time to time.
2. Then turn off the heat, and immediately sprinkle the erythritol and cinnamon over the top, and stir to distribute. (If you wait for the nuts to cool, the sweetener doesn't stick nearly as well.)

Nutrition: 239 Calories | Fat: 24g | Protein: 5g | Carbohydrates: 5g

Cream Cheese Balls

 Prep Time: 10 minutes Cook Time: 8 minutes Servings: 8

Ingredients

- Eight ounces of cream cheese, chilled
- One package (0.3 ounces) of sugar-free gelatin, any flavor

Directions

1. Cut your bar of cream cheese into 16 equal chunks. Use clean hands to roll each into a ball.
2. Pour the gelatin onto a plate, and roll each ball in the powder to coat. That's it.
3. Store these in an airtight container in the fridge.

Nutrition: 103 Calories | Fat: 10g | Protein: 1g | Carbohydrates: 0g

Glazed Walnuts

 Prep Time: 10 minutes Cook Time: 10 minutes Servings: 6

Ingredients

- One and a half cups of walnuts
- Boiling water, as needed
- Half teaspoon of vanilla extract
- One tablespoon of erythritol
- Coconut oil, for frying

Directions

1. Put your walnuts in a bowl, and cover them with boiling water. Let them sit for just 4 or 5 minutes, then drain well.
2. Add the vanilla, and toss till it's evenly distributed. Add the erythritol, and toss until they're all evenly coated.
3. Now spread your walnuts on a plate, and let them dry for an hour or two. This will minimize spitting when you fry them.
4. Put your big, heavy skillet over medium heat, and add 1/4 inch (6 mm) of coconut oil.
5. Let it get hot, then fry your walnuts a handful at a time, till just crisp.
6. Cool, and store in a tightly lidded container.

Nutrition: 191 Calories | Fat: 18g | Protein: 4g | Carbohydrates: 2g

Flan

Ingredients

- Two cups of heavy cream
- 1/3 cup of erythritol
- One teaspoon of vanilla extract
- Half teaspoon of liquid stevia* (vanilla)
- Six eggs
- Pinch of salt
- Pinch of ground nutmeg
- Eight tablespoons of sugar-free caramel coffee flavoring syrup

Prep Time: 10 minutes **Cook Time:** 1 h 15 min **Servings:** 8

Directions

1. Preheat the oven to 350°F.
2. Grease a 10-inch (25 cm) pie plate or a nine-and-a-half-inch (24 cm) deep-dish pie plate.
3. Put the cream, erythritol, vanilla, stevia, eggs, salt, and nutmeg in your blender, and run till it's all well combined.
4. Put a shallow baking pan on the oven rack. Place the prepared pie plate in it. Pour water in the outer pan up to about half an inch (1 cm) of the rim of the pie plate. Now pour the custard mixture into the pie plate.
5. Bake for 50 to 60 minutes, or until just set.
6. Carefully remove the pie plate from the water bath to let it cool for 30 minutes before chilling.
7. You can run a knife around the edge and invert the flan onto a plate, then top with the caramel syrup to serve, but it's easier to just cut wedges like a pie or spoon it out. Still, top it with the syrup to serve!

Nutrition: 256 Calories | Fat: 25g | Protein: 5g | Carbohydrates: 2g

Merry Crispness Shortbread

Ingredients

- 2/3 cup of vanilla whey protein powder
- 2/3 cup of almond meal
- One teaspoon of xanthan or guar
- Half cup of butter at room temperature
- Half cup of coconut oil—solid, not melted—but not chilled and rock hard
- A quarter cup of powdered erythritol, plus extra for dusting
- Half teaspoon of salt
- One egg yolk
- One and 1/3 cups of shredded coconut meat (unsweetened)

Prep Time: 10 minutes **Cook Time:** 35 minutes **Servings:** 48 cookies

Directions

1. Preheat the oven to 325°F.
2. Line a jelly roll pan with baking parchment.
3. In a bowl, whisk together the protein powder, almond meal, and xanthan so they're evenly distributed.
4. In another bowl, using your electric mixer, beat the butter and coconut oil together until they're fluffy and creamy.
5. Beat in the erythritol and salt, mixing till it's completely blended—scrape down the sides of the bowl as needed. Now beat in the egg yolk.
6. Beat in the almond meal mixture in 3 additions, making sure each is well blended before adding more. Finally, beat in the shredded coconut.
7. Turn the dough out onto the parchment-lined jelly roll pan. Place another sheet of parchment over it, and using a rolling pin and your hands, press the dough out into an even sheet, completely covering the pan.
8. When you have a beautiful rectangle of dough, peel off the top parchment and use a thin, straight-bladed knife to score it into squares.
9. Bake for 10 to 12 minutes, until golden. Keep an eye on it—it goes from golden to over-browned quickly.
10. When your shortbread comes out of the oven, re-score it, then use a sifter to dust it with a little more erythritol.
11. Let your shortbread cool in the pan, then use a pancake turner to transfer it to an airtight container or cookie tin.

Nutrition: 66 Calories | Fat: 6g | Protein: 3g | Carbohydrates: 1g

Hazelnut Shortbread

 Prep Time: 10 minutes
 Cook Time: 50 minutes
 Servings: 48 cookies

Ingredients

- Two cups of hazelnuts
- One cup of vanilla whey protein powder
- Half teaspoon of salt
- A quarter teaspoon of baking powder
- One cup of butter, at room temperature
- Half cup of powdered erythritol
- One egg
- Two tablespoons of water

Directions

1. Preheat the oven to 325°F.
2. First, grind the hazelnuts to a fine meal in a food processor. Add the vanilla whey protein, salt, and baking powder, and pulse to combine.
3. Using an electric mixer, beat the butter until it's fluffy. Add the erythritol and beat well again. Next, beat in the egg, again combining well. Now beat in the hazelnut mixture in 3 or 4 additions. Finally, beat in the water.
4. You will now have a soft, sticky dough. Line a shallow baking pan—a jelly roll pan is best; mine is 14 and a half × 15 Half inches (29 × 39 cm)—with baking parchment, and turn the dough out onto the parchment. Cover it with another piece of parchment, and through the top sheet, press the dough out into an even layer covering the whole pan. It should be about 1/4 inch (6 mm) thick.
5. Peel off the top sheet of parchment, and use a knife with a nonserrated, thin blade to score the dough into squares.
6. Bake for 25 to 30 minutes or until golden.
7. You'll need to re-score the lines before removing the shortbread from the pan—use a straight up-and-down motion, and the shortbread will be less likely to break.

Nutrition: 91 Calories | Fat: 8g | Protein: 5g | Carbohydrates: 1g

Lemon-Cheese Mousse

 Prep Time: 10 minutes
 Cook Time: 15 minutes
 Servings: 8

Ingredients

- Two tablespoons of cold water
- One tablespoon of unflavored gelatin
- A quarter cup of lemon juice
- Four egg whites
- A quarter teaspoon of cream of tartar
- Eight ounces of cream cheese
- A quarter teaspoon of liquid stevia (lemon drop), or more to taste
- One egg
- Half cup of sour cream
- One teaspoon of grated lemon zest

Directions

1. First, put the water in a small cup, and sprinkle the gelatin on top to soften. Let that sit for 10 minutes.
2. Meanwhile, put your lemon juice in a small, nonreactive saucepan over low heat, and warm it up. When the gelatin is softened, add it to the lemon juice, and stir until the gelatin is completely dissolved and there are no granules left.
3. Now you need to beat your egg whites. Make sure the bowl and the beaters are completely grease-free and that there's not even a tiny speck of yolk in your egg whites, or they won't whip! Beat them until they're frothy, then add the cream of tartar, and beat until stiff peaks form. Set aside for a minute or two while you do the next step.
4. In a mixing bowl, use your electric mixer to beat the cream cheese with the stevia and egg until it's light and fluffy. Now beat in the sour cream, lemon zest, and gelatin mixture.
5. Gently fold this cream cheese mixture into the egg whites. Now pour the mousse into eight pretty dessert dishes, and chill for at least 4 to 6 hours before serving.

Nutrition: 156 Calories | Fat: 13g | Protein: 5g | Carbohydrates: 4g

Italian Walnut Cake

Prep Time: 10 minutes
Cook Time: 55 minutes
Servings: 12

Ingredients

- Twelve ounces of walnuts
- Half cup of erythritol, divided
- Four eggs
- Pinch of cream of tartar
- 1/3 teaspoon of EZ-Sweetz Family Size
- Two teaspoons of lemon zest
- Pinch of salt
- Two tablespoons of powdered erythritol for topping

Directions

1. Preheat the oven to 350°F.
2. Coat a 9-inch (23 cm) springform pan with non-stick cooking spray, and line the bottom with a circle of baking parchment or a reusable non-stick pan liner.
3. Put the walnuts in your food processor with the S-blade in place. Pulse till the nuts are chopped medium-fine. Add two tablespoons of the erythritol, and pulse until the nuts are finely ground but not oily. (Don't overprocess. You don't want nut butter!)
4. Separate your eggs. Since even the tiniest speck of egg yolk will cause the whites to stubbornly refuse to whip, do yourself a big favor and separate each one into a small dish or cup before adding the white to the bowl you plan to whip them in!
5. Then, if you break a yolk, you've only messed up that white. Put the whites in a deep, narrow mixing bowl, and put the yolks in a larger mixing bowl.
6. Add the pinch of cream of tartar to the whites, and using your electric mixer (not a blender or food processor), whip the egg whites until they stand in stiff peaks. Set aside.
7. In a larger bowl, beat the yolks with the remaining six tablespoons (90 g) erythritol, and all of the EZ-Sweetz, until the mixture is pale yellow and very creamy—at least 3 to 4 minutes. Beat in the lemon zest and the salt.
8. Stir the ground walnuts into the yolk mixture—you can use the electric mixer, but the mixture will be thick. When that's well combined, gently fold in the egg whites one-third at a time, using a rubber scraper.
9. Incorporate each third well before adding the next third. When all the egg whites are folded in, gently pour the batter into the prepared pan.
10. Bake for 45 minutes. Sprinkle the top with the two tablespoons of powdered erythritol while the cake is hot, then let cool before serving.
11. Cut into thin wedges to serve.

Nutrition: 195 Calories | Fat: 18g | Protein: 9g | Carbohydrates: 4g

Marbled Cheesecake Muffins

Ingredients

For muffins
- Five eggs
- Sixteen ounces of full-fat ricotta
- Eight ounces of cream cheese softened
- One cup of Splenda
- One teaspoon of almond extract
- Half teaspoon of vanilla extract
- One and a half tablespoons of unsweetened cocoa powder

For topping
- Half cup of sour cream
- One tablespoon of Splenda
- A quarter teaspoon of vanilla extract

 Prep Time: 10 minutes   Cook Time: 40 minutes   Servings: 12

Directions

1. Preheat the oven to 350°F.
2. To make the muffins, in a medium bowl with an electric mixer, beat the eggs briefly until blended. Add the rest of the muffin ingredients, except the cocoa, to the bowl, and beat until completely blended.
3. Pour into muffin pans lined with cupcake liners until about one-fifth of the batter remains in the bowl.
4. Add the cocoa powder to the remaining batter (there is no need to worry about or be exact with the amount of batter leftover in the bowl; this recipe is very forgiving). Mix it in.
5. Slowly pour a dollop of the cocoa batter into the center of each cupcake so that you have a two-toned design. Bake for 30 to 35 minutes until the top is puffy and slightly cracked and a toothpick inserted into the center comes out relatively clean.
6. Remove the cupcakes from the oven to cool for a few minutes.
7. To make the topping, while the cupcakes are cooling, mix the topping ingredients together.
8. Drop a rounded teaspoon of the topping onto the center of each cupcake (no need to flatten or shape) and return to the oven for another 5 minutes.
9. Cool and keep refrigerated. These freeze wonderfully, so you can always have some on hand.

Nutrition: 182 Calories | Fat: 15g | Protein: 8g | Carbohydrates: 3g

Mixed Berry Cups

 Prep Time: 10 minutes   Cook Time: 0 minutes   Servings: 6

Directions

1. Put the gelatin, water, lemon juice, and orange zest in a blender, and whirl for 10 to 15 seconds to dissolve the gelatin.
2. Add the blackberries, and whirl again, just long enough to blend in the berries.
3. Put the blender container in the refrigerator for 10 minutes—just until the mixture starts to thicken a bit.
4. Add 3/4 cup of the heavy cream, and run the blender just long enough to mix it all in—about 10 to 15 seconds.
5. Pour into six pretty little dessert cups and chill. Whip the remaining quarter cup of cream with the vanilla liquid stevia, and dollop a spoonful on each serving for garnish.

Nutrition: 156 Calories | Fat: 15g | Protein: 1g | Carbohydrates: 5g

Ingredients

- One package (0.3 ounces) of sugar-free raspberry gelatin
- One cup of boiling water
- Two teaspoons of lemon juice
- Grated zest of half orange (feed the orange to the kids)
- 3/4 cup of frozen blackberries, partly thawed
- One cup of heavy cream, divided
- Twelve drops of liquid stevia (vanilla)

Merry Crispness Shortbread

Ingredients

- 2/3 cup of vanilla whey protein powder
- 2/3 cup of almond meal
- One teaspoon of xanthan or guar
- Half cup of butter at room temperature
- Half cup of coconut oil—solid, not melted—but not chilled and rock hard
- A quarter cup of powdered erythritol, plus extra for dusting
- Half teaspoon of salt
- One egg yolk
- One and 1/3 cups of shredded coconut meat (unsweetened)

 Prep Time: 10 minutes   Cook Time: 35 minutes   Servings: 48 cookies

Directions

1. Preheat the oven to 325°F.
2. Line a jelly roll pan with baking parchment.
3. In a bowl, whisk together the protein powder, almond meal, and xanthan so they're evenly distributed.
4. In another bowl, using your electric mixer, beat the butter and coconut oil together until they're fluffy and creamy.
5. Beat in the erythritol and salt, mixing till it's completely blended—scrape down the sides of the bowl as needed. Now beat in the egg yolk.
6. Beat in the almond meal mixture in 3 additions, making sure each is well blended before adding more. Finally, beat in the shredded coconut.
7. Turn the dough out onto the parchment-lined jelly roll pan. Place another sheet of parchment over it, and using a rolling pin and your hands, press the dough out into an even sheet, completely covering the pan.
8. When you have a beautiful rectangle of dough, peel off the top parchment and use a thin, straight-bladed knife to score it into squares.
9. Bake for 10 to 12 minutes, until golden. Keep an eye on it—it goes from golden to over-browned quickly.
10. When your shortbread comes out of the oven, re-score it, then use a sifter to dust it with a little more erythritol.
11. Let your shortbread cool in the pan, then use a pancake turner to transfer it to an airtight container or cookie tin.

Nutrition: 66 Calories | Fat: 6g | Protein: 3g | Carbohydrates: 1g

Pumpkin Cheesecake

Ingredients

- Two pounds of cream cheese at room temperature
- One cup of canned pumpkin puree (not pumpkin pie filling)
- Three tablespoons of heavy cream
- One teaspoon of EZ-Sweetz Family Size
- One teaspoon of ground cinnamon
- One teaspoon of ground ginger
- Half teaspoon of ground nutmeg
- Five eggs

 Prep Time: 10 minutes   Cook Time: 1 h 30 min   Servings: 10

Directions

1. Preheat the oven to 375°F.
2. Line a 9-inch (23 cm) springform pan with non-stick foil, covering the seam at the bottom. Butter the whole thing well, bottom and sides, or coat with non-stick cooking spray.
3. Simply put all your ingredients in a big mixing bowl, and beat with an electric mixer until it's all smoothly blended.
4. Pour into the prepared pan.
5. Place in the oven. Put a roasting pan with 1 inch (2.5 cm) of water in the oven on the rack beneath.
6. Bake the cheesecake for 10 minutes. Reduce the heat to 250°F and bake for an additional hour.
7. At the end of the hour, remove the cake and run a knife around the edge of the pan.
8. Return the cheesecake to the warm oven and let it sit until the oven cools (approximately another hour).
9. Chill in the fridge overnight and enjoy!

Nutrition: 375 Calories | Fat: 36g | Protein: 10g | Carbohydrates: 5g

Juice and Smoothies Recipes

Apricot-Orange Smoothie

Prep Time: 10 minutes Cook Time: 0 minutes Servings: 2

Directions

1. Combine the coconut milk, apricots, orange, lemon juice, rose water, if using, and ice in a blender and pulse until smooth.
2. Add the gelatin and pulse again until smooth. Pour into two 8-ounce glasses and enjoy.

Nutrition: 119 Calories | Fat: 2g | Proteins-8g | Carbohydrates: 8g

Ingredients

- Two cups of full-fat, canned coconut milk
- Two medium apricots pitted
- One large navel orange, peeled
- One tablespoon of lemon juice
- One teaspoon of rose water
- Two cups of ice
- Two tablespoons of grass-fed beef gelatin

Beet Greens Smoothie

Prep Time: 10 minutes Cook Time: 0 minutes Servings: 2

Directions

1. Combine all the ingredients together in a food processor.
2. Pulse it two to three times.
3. Serve and enjoy.

Nutrition: 51 Calories | Fat: 2g | Proteins-0.3g | Carbohydrates: 8g

Ingredients

- One cup of Beet Greens
- Two tablespoons of Pumpkin seeds butter
- One cup of Strawberry
- One tablespoon of sesame seeds
- One tablespoon of hemp seeds
- One cup of chamomile tea

Broccoli Apple Smoothie

Prep Time: 10 minutes   Cook Time: 0 minutes   Servings: 2

Directions

1. Combine all the ingredients together in a food processor.
2. Pulse it two to three times.
3. Serve and enjoy.

Nutrition: 89 Calories | Fat: 2g | Proteins-4g | Carbohydrates: 7g

Ingredients

- One Apple
- One cup of Broccoli
- One tablespoon of Cilantro
- One Celery stalk
- One cup of crushed ice
- One tablespoon of crushed Seaweed

Dandelion Smoothie

Ingredients

- One cup of Dandelion greens
- One cup of Spinach
- Half cup of tahini
- One Red Radish
- One tablespoon of chia seeds
- One cup of lavender tea

Prep Time: 10 minutes   Cook Time: 0 minutes   Servings: 2

Directions

1. Combine all the ingredients together in a food processor.
2. Pulse it two to three times.
3. Serve and enjoy.

Nutrition: 56 Calories | Fat: 0.2g | Proteins-0.3g | Carbohydrates: 9g

Flax Almond Butter Smoothie

Ingredients

- Half cup of plain yogurt
- Two tablespoons of almond butter
- Two cups of spinach
- Three strawberries
- Half cup of crushed ice
- One teaspoon of flax seeds

Prep Time: 10 minutes   Cook Time: 0 minutes   Servings: 2

Directions

1. Combine all the ingredients in a food processor.
2. Pulse it two to three times.
3. Serve and enjoy.

Nutrition: 119 Calories | Fat: 2g | Proteins-8g | Carbohydrates: 8g

Kale Kiwi Smoothie

 Prep Time: 10 minutes   Cook Time: 0 minutes   Servings: 2

Directions

1. Combine all the ingredients in a food processor.
2. Pulse it two to three times.
3. Serve and enjoy.

Nutrition: 89 Calories | Fat: 2g | Proteins-4g | Carbohydrates: 5g

Ingredients

- One cup of kale, chopped
- One Apple
- Two Kiwis
- One tablespoon of flax seeds
- One tablespoon of lucuma powder
- One cup of crushed ice

Pineapple Raspberry Smoothie

 Prep Time: 20 minutes   Cook Time: 15 minutes   Servings: 2

Directions

1. A piece of pineapple peels and removes the core. Cut into medium pieces.
2. Raspberries can be put frozen and can be thawed overnight on the top shelf of the refrigerator.
3. Take one cup of rice milk (in the absence, of course, you can replace it with non-fat milk), buckwheat flakes, slices of mandarin, and pineapple, and beat at high speed in a blender.
4. Let stand for about 10-15 minutes. During this time, buckwheat flakes will swell.
5. Add another quarter cup of rice drink and punch in the blender again. If the smoothie is still thick, bring the water or rice drink to the desired concentration.
6. Garnish with fresh mint leaves.

Nutrition: 50 Calories | Proteins-8g | Fat: 0.5g | Carbohydrates: 8g

Ingredients

- One and a half lb. of pineapple
- Ten ounces of frozen raspberries
- One and a quarter cups of vanilla rice milk
- Three tablespoons of buckwheat flakes
- Mint to taste

Pomegranate-Blueberry Smoothie

 Prep Time: 10 minutes   Cook Time: 0 min   Servings: 2

Directions

1. Place the coconut milk and pomegranate seeds in a blender and blend until almost smooth (there will still be small bits of seed).
2. Pour the mixture through a wire-mesh strainer set over a bowl, pressing against the seeds to extract as much liquid as possible. Discard the seeds.
3. Rinse out the blender. Pour the strained coconut and pomegranate mixture into the blender and add the rose water, blueberries, and honey.
4. Pulse a few more seconds, add the gelatin, and pulse until smooth. Pour into two 8-ounce glasses and enjoy.

Nutrition: 121 Calories | Fat: 8g | Proteins-12g | Carbohydrates: 5g

Ingredients

- Two cups of full-fat, canned coconut milk
- One cup of pomegranate seeds
- One tablespoon of rose water or grated orange zest
- Two cups of frozen blueberries
- One tablespoon of honey
- Two tablespoons of grass-fed beef gelatin

Summer Rhubarb Cooler

 Prep Time: 10 minutes   Cook Time: 10 minutes   Servings: 2

Directions

1. Bring sweetener and water to a boil in a large saucepan over high heat. Cook, often stirring, to dissolve sugar for about 2 minutes.
2. Reduce heat to medium and add rhubarb, then cook until tender. Add strawberries and lemon juice and cook for two additional minutes.
3. Strain the mixture through a sieve to remove solids. Pour strained mixture into a 9x13-inch baking dish, cover with plastic wrap, and place in the freezer. Every 30 minutes, stir the mixture with the tips of the fork to break up any forming ice chunks.
4. Freeze mixture until slushy and frozen, about 3 hours. When frozen, scoop into chilled glasses and garnish with remaining sliced strawberries.

Nutrition: 35 Calories | Proteins-0g | Fat: 2g | Carbohydrates: 7g

Ingredients

- A quarter cup of low-calorie baking sweetener
- One cup of water
- Half pound of fresh rhubarb, trimmed and cut into 1-inch pieces
- One cup of sliced fresh strawberries plus extra for garnish
- Three tablespoons of freshly squeezed lemon juice
- Drinking glasses chilled in the freezer

Zucchini Apples Smoothie

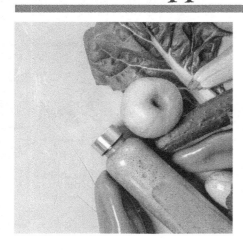

 Prep Time: 10 minutes

 Cook Time: 0 minutes

 Servings: 2

Directions

1. Combine all the ingredients in a food processor.
2. Pulse it two to three times.
3. Serve and enjoy.

Nutrition: 99 Calories | Fat: 4g | Proteins-8g | Carbohydrates: 7g

Ingredients

- Half cup of zucchini
- One Apple
- 3/4 avocado
- One stalk Celery
- One Lemon
- One tablespoon of Spirulina
- One and a half cups of crushed ice

Meal plan (21 Weeks)

Week 1

	Breakfast	Lunch	Snack	Dinner
Day 1	Coconut flax bread	Stracciatella	One and a half ounces of dried apricots	Chicken-chili-cheese salad
Day 2	raunschweiger omelette	Classic spinach salad	One rye cracker spread with ¾ ounce of low-fat soft chees	Meatza
Day 3	Coconut flax bread	Frijoles Charros	One and a half ounces of dried apricots	Spinach-plum salad
Day 4	Perfect protein pancakes	Pork loin with red wine and walnuts	One pear	Egg drop soup
Day 5	Buffalo wing omelet	Pepperoncini spinach	Two sticks of celery filled with One and ¾ ounces of low-fat sof	Golden triangle chicken kabobs
Day 6	Asparagus with Egg	Super-easy turkey divan	Reduced-fat whole grain cookie	Classic spinach salad
Day 7	Smoked salmon and goat cheese scramble	Smothered burgers	One and a half ounces of dried apricots	Goulash

Week 2

	Breakfast	Lunch	Snack	Dinner
Day 1	Confetti frittata	Sweet-and-sour cabbage	One apple	Zucchini meat loaf Italiano
Day 2	Confetti frittata	Shrimp Caesar Salad	One rye cracker spread with ¾ ounce of low-fat soft chees	Balsamic-glazed chicken and peppers
Day 3	Greek cheese, spinach, and olive omelet	Slow-cooker pork chili	Low-fat fruit yogurt	Sun-dried tomato-portobello salmon roast
Day 4	Coconut flax bread	Glazed salmon	Reduced-fat whole grain cookie	Banh mi Burgers
Day 5	Insta-quiche	Smothered burgers	One banana	Sopa tlalpeñ
Day 6	California omelet	Chicken in creamy orange sauce	One pear	Cream of mushroom soup
Day 7	Fried mush	Old Fashioned Salmon Soup	One small banana	Baked clams

Week 3

	Breakfast	Lunch	Snack	Dinner
Day 1	Coconut flax bread	Bacon, tomato, and cauliflower salad	Reduced-fat whole grain cookie	Sautéed sesame spinac
Day 2	Asparagus with Egg	Salmon with pesto mayonnaise	Two sticks of celery filled with One and ¾ ounces of low-fat soft chees	Not-quite-middle-eastern salad
Day 3	Smoked salmon and goat cheese scramble	Chicken-chili-cheese salad	Two sticks of celery filled with One and ¾ ounces of low-fat soft chees	Joe (Beef)
Day 4	Coconut flax bread	Salmon with pesto mayonnaise	One apple	Gingered monkfish
Day 5	Fried mush	Glazed salmon	Seven ounces of skim milk	Chicken breasts stuffed with artichokes and garlic cheese
Day 6	Backward pizza	Poached trout with dill	One and a half ounces of dried apricots	Cranberry-peach turkey roast
Day 7	Rodeo eggs	Lamb, feta, and spinach burgers	One rye cracker spread with ¾ ounce of low-fat soft chees	Minestrone

Week 4

	Breakfast	Lunch	Snack	Dinner
Day 1	Backward pizza	Lamb, feta, and spinach burgers	Reduced-fat whole grain cookie	Beef Stroganoff
Day 2	Braunschweiger omelette	Hummus	Low-fat fruit yogurt	Maple-spice country-style ribs
Day 3	Pork rind waffles	Chicken in creamy orange sauce	Two sticks of celery filled with One and ¾ ounces of low-fat sof	Olive soup
Day 4	Pork rind waffles	Lamb, feta, and spinach burgers	One low-fat/low-sugar cereal bar	Garbanzo Stir Fry
Day 5	Quork	Baked clams	Two sticks of celery filled with One and ¾ ounces of low-fat soft chees	Shrimp Caesar Salad
Day 6	Club omelet	Roasted curried cauliflower	Two sticks of celery filled with One and ¾ ounces of low-fat soft chees	Egg salad
Day 7	Rosemary cheese crackers	Rib-eye steak with wine sauce	One rye cracker spread with ¾ ounce of low-fat soft chees	Bacon, tomato, and cauliflower salad

Week 5

	Breakfast	Lunch	Snack	Dinner
Day 1	Insta-quiche	Skillet citrus chicken	One banana	Japanese fried rice
Day 2	Insta-quiche	Mushrooms with bacon, sun-dried tomatoes, and cheese	One low-fat/low-sugar cereal bar	Classic spinach salad
Day 3	Coconut flax bread	Chicken burgers with basil and sun-dried tomatoes	One rye cracker spread with ¾ ounce of low-fat soft chees	Dilled chicken salad
Day 4	Coconut flax bread	Mushroom risotto	Two sticks of celery filled with One and ¾ ounces of low-fat sof	Chicken in creamy horseradish sauce
Day 5	Asparagus with Egg	Golden triangle chicken kabobs	One banana	Chicken in creamy horseradish sauce
Day 6	California omelet	Bourbon-maple glazed pork chops	One rye cracker spread with ¾ ounce of low-fat soft chees	Poor man's poivra
Day 7	California omelet	Tavern soup	One orange	Asian ginger slaw

Week 6

	Breakfast	Lunch	Snack	Dinner
Day 1	Rosemary cheese crackers	Mushroom risotto	Two sticks of celery filled with One and ¾ ounces of low-fat sof	Bacon, tomato, and cauliflower salad
Day 2	Monterey jack and avocado omelet	Sautéed sesame spinac	Seven ounces of skim milk	Not-quite-middle-eastern salad
Day 3	Rodeo eggs	Smothered burgers	Reduced-fat whole grain cookie	Glazed salmon
Day 4	Backward pizza	Mustard-maple glazed pork steak	One and a half ounces of dried apricots	Garbanzo Stir Fry
Day 5	Braunschweiger omelette	Glazed salmon	One apple	Hazelnut green beans
Day 6	Parmesan-rosemary eggs	Beef and bacon rice with pine nuts	Low-fat fruit yogurt	Middle eastern marinated lamb kabobs
Day 7	Club omelet	Crab and asparagus soup	One apple	Toasted salad

Week 7

	Breakfast	Lunch	Snack	Dinner
Day 1	Salted caramel–cinnamon pancak	Asparagus with mushrooms and hazelnuts	One small banana	Glazed salmon
Day 2	California omelet	Lemon-herb chicken breast	Two sticks of celery filled with One and ¾ ounces of low-fat soft chees	Chicken burgers with basil and sun-dried tomatoes
Day 3	Unpotato tortilla	Spinach-plum salad	One small banana	Egg drop soup
Day 4	Monterey jack and avocado omelet	Japanese fried rice	Low-fat fruit yogurt	Chicken-pecan salad
Day 5	Salted caramel–cinnamon pancak	Chicken-pecan salad	Seven ounces of skim milk	Pepperoncini beef
Day 6	Pork rind waffles	Lemon-herb chicken breast	One rye cracker spread with ¾ ounce of low-fat soft chees	Pesto shrimp
Day 7	Monterey jack and avocado omelet	Pan-broiled steak	One banana	Chicken-pecan salad

Week 8

	Breakfast	Lunch	Snack	Dinner
Day 1	Braunschweiger omelette	Tokyo ginger pork chops	Low-fat fruit yogurt	Chicken-almond noodle salad
Day 2	Pork rind waffles	Dilled chicken salad	One pear	Banh mi Burgers
Day 3	Salted caramel–cinnamon pancak	Roman lamb steak	One pear	Sweet-and-sour cabbage
Day 4	Confetti frittata	Olive soup	One low-fat/low-sugar cereal bar	Mustard-grilled pork with balsamic onions
Day 5	Salted caramel–cinnamon pancak	Chicken skewers Diavolo	One low-fat/low-sugar cereal bar	Frijoles Charros
Day 6	Asparagus with Egg	Poor man's poivra	Seven ounces of skim milk	Minestrone
Day 7	Pork rind waffles	Steak au poivre with brandy cream	Reduced-fat whole grain cookie	Asian ginger slaw

Week 9

	Breakfast	Lunch	Snack	Dinner
Day 1	Quork	Old Fashioned Salmon Soup	Two sticks of celery filled with One and ¾ ounces of low-fat sof	Asparagus with soy and sesame mayonnaise
Day 2	Buffalo wing omelet	Egg drop soup	One banana	Olive soup
Day 3	Perfect protein pancakes	Lemon-herb chicken breast	One apple	Kalua pig with cabbage
Day 4	Braunschweiger omelette	Two-cheese cauliflower	One pear	Sirloin with Anaheim-lime marinade
Day 5	Fried mush	Tuna salad	One orange	Hazelnut green beans
Day 6	Asparagus with Egg	Mustard-maple glazed pork steak	One small banana	Crab and asparagus soup
Day 7	Backward pizza	Pan-broiled steak	One low-fat/low-sugar cereal bar	Avocado and brown rice sala

Week 10

	Breakfast	Lunch	Snack	Dinner
Day 1	Asparagus with Egg	Classic spinach salad	Low-fat fruit yogurt	Lemon-herb chicken breast
Day 2	California omelet	Cheddar-broccoli salad	One small banana	Hazelnut green beans
Day 3	Pork rind waffles	Roasted cauliflower with Tahini sauce	Low-fat fruit yogurt	Crab and asparagus soup
Day 4	Monterey scramble	Turkey with mushroom sauce	One banana	Mustard-grilled pork with balsamic onions
Day 5	Coconut flax bread	Tavern soup	Two sticks of celery filled with One and ¾ ounces of low-fat sof	Sesame-asparagus salad
Day 6	Backward pizza	Sirloin with Anaheim-lime marinade	One rye cracker spread with ¾ ounce of low-fat soft chees	Glazed salmon
Day 7	Fried mush	Asian ginger slaw	One rye cracker spread with ¾ ounce of low-fat soft chees	Chicken Caesar salad

Week 11

	Breakfast	Lunch	Snack	Dinner
Day 1	Greek cheese, spinach, and olive omelet	Chicken-almond noodle salad	One low-fat/low-sugar cereal bar	Bleu burger
Day 2	Braunschweiger omelette	Japanese fried rice	One low-fat/low-sugar cereal bar	Kalua pig with cabbage
Day 3	Buffalo wing omelet	Joe (Beef)	One pear	Lamb, feta, and spinach burgers
Day 4	Backward pizza	Roman stew	Two sticks of celery filled with One and ¾ ounces of low-fat sof	Cranberry-peach turkey roast
Day 5	Rodeo eggs	Hazelnut green beans	Two sticks of celery filled with One and ¾ ounces of low-fat sof	Sweet-and-sour cabbage
Day 6	Smoked salmon and goat cheese scramble	Beef Stroganoff	One orange	Transcendent flounder
Day 7	Rodeo eggs	Cream of salmon soup	One pear	Cranberry-peach turkey roast

Week 12

	Breakfast	Lunch	Snack	Dinner
Day 1	Parmesan-rosemary eggs	Egg salad	One orange	Asian ginger slaw
Day 2	Backward pizza	Pepperoncini beef	Two sticks of celery filled with One and ¾ ounces of low-fat sof	Zucchini meat loaf Italiano
Day 3	Coconut flax bread	Chicken in creamy horseradish sauce	One apple	Tandoori chicken
Day 4	Buffalo wing omelet	Tuna salad with lemon and capers	One orange	Chicken in creamy orange sauce
Day 5	Perfect protein pancakes	Bleu burger	Two sticks of celery filled with One and ¾ ounces of low-fat soft chees	Mustard-grilled pork with balsamic onions
Day 6	Salted caramel–cinnamon pancak	Chicken skewers Diavolo	Two sticks of celery filled with One and ¾ ounces of low-fat soft chees	Asparagus with soy and sesame mayonnaise
Day 7	Greek cheese, spinach, and olive omelet	Bacon, tomato, and cauliflower salad	Reduced-fat whole grain cookie	Yucatán chicke

Week 13

	Breakfast	Lunch	Snack	Dinner
Day 1	California omelet	Salmon with pesto mayonnaise	Two sticks of celery filled with One and ¾ ounces of low-fat sof	Cauliflower puré
Day 2	Parmesan-rosemary eggs	Maple-spice country-style ribs	One banana	Mustard-grilled pork with balsamic onions
Day 3	Pork rind waffles	Garbanzo Stir Fry	Two sticks of celery filled with One and ¾ ounces of low-fat soft chees	Olive soup
Day 4	Asparagus with Egg	Chicken-chili-cheese salad	One rye cracker spread with ¾ ounce of low-fat soft chees	Mediterranean lamb burgers
Day 5	Pork rind waffles	Minestrone	One and a half ounces of dried apricots	Maple-spice country-style ribs
Day 6	California omelet	Egg drop soup	One apple	Minestrone
Day 7	Coconut flax bread	Lemon-herb zucchini	One and a half ounces of dried apricots	Roman stew

Week 14

	Breakfast	Lunch	Snack	Dinner
Day 1	Parmesan-rosemary eggs	Chinese-style tuna soup	One small banana	Asian ginger slaw
Day 2	Smoked salmon and goat cheese scramble	Thanksgiving weekend curry	One and a half ounces of dried apricots	Meatza
Day 3	Greek cheese, spinach, and olive omelet	Sun-dried tomato-portobello salmon roast	One low-fat/low-sugar cereal bar	Chili-bacon scallops
Day 4	Braunschweiger omelette	Frijoles Charros	One and a half ounces of dried apricots	Hummus
Day 5	Rodeo eggs	Lamb steaks with lemon, olives, and capers	Seven ounces of skim milk	Cauli-rice
Day 6	Rosemary cheese crackers	Creamy Broccoli Soup	One apple	Shrimp Caesar Salad
Day 7	Parmesan-rosemary eggs	Cucumber-wrapped vegetable rolls	One banana	Shrimp Caesar Salad

Week 15

	Breakfast	Lunch	Snack	Dinner
Day 1	Parmesan-rosemary eggs	Poached trout with dill	Two sticks of celery filled with One and ¾ ounces of low-fat soft chees	Gingered monkfish
Day 2	Asparagus with Egg	Roman stew	Seven ounces of skim milk	Unpotato salad
Day 3	Quork	Pepperoncini beef	One rye cracker spread with ¾ ounce of low-fat soft chees	Egg salad
Day 4	Insta-quiche	Chard and Cashew Saut<c3>	One small banana	Egg salad
Day 5	Monterey jack and avocado omelet	Crab and asparagus soup	Two sticks of celery filled with One and ¾ ounces of low-fat soft chees	Hazelnut green beans
Day 6	Parmesan-rosemary eggs	Spareribs Adobado	One orange	Rib-eye steak with wine sauce
Day 7	Greek cheese, spinach, and olive omelet	Chicken burgers with basil and sun-dried tomatoes	One banana	Lemon-herb zucchini

Week 16

	Breakfast	Lunch	Snack	Dinner
Day 1	California omelet	Baked clams	One apple	Chili-bacon scallops
Day 2	Coconut flax bread	Not-quite-middle-eastern salad	Low-fat fruit yogurt	Maple-chipotle glazed pork steaks
Day 3	Quork	Bourbon-maple glazed pork chops	One rye cracker spread with ¾ ounce of low-fat soft chees	Turkey with mushroom sauce
Day 4	Parmesan-rosemary eggs	Salmon with pesto mayonnaise	Reduced-fat whole grain cookie	Mediterranean lamb burgers
Day 5	Rodeo eggs	Rib-eye steak with wine sauce	One low-fat/low-sugar cereal bar	Skillet citrus chicken
Day 6	Club omelet	Asian ginger slaw	One low-fat/low-sugar cereal bar	Kalua pig with cabbage
Day 7	Confetti frittata	Pepperoncini spinach	One small banana	Braised Green Beans with Pork

Week 17

	Breakfast	Lunch	Snack	Dinner
Day 1	California omelet	Pan-broiled steak	One orange	Gorgonzola-and-pesto Caesar salad
Day 2	Insta-quiche	Chicken-chili-cheese salad	Reduced-fat whole grain cookie	Zucchini meat loaf Italiano
Day 3	Fried mush	Sopa tlalpeñ	One orange	Gingered monkfish
Day 4	Asparagus with Egg	Balsamic-glazed chicken and peppers	Seven ounces of skim milk	Stracciatella
Day 5	Insta-quiche	Poor man's poivra	One low-fat/low-sugar cereal bar	Cauliflower puré
Day 6	Braunschweiger omelette	Minestrone	One banana	Cream of salmon soup
Day 7	Club omelet	Roasted asparagus	One pear	Pork with a camembert sauce

Week 18

	Breakfast	Lunch	Snack	Dinner
Day 1	Coconut flax bread	Salmon with pesto mayonnaise	One apple	Lamb steaks with lemon, olives, and capers
Day 2	Quork	Cheddar-broccoli salad	One and a half ounces of dried apricots	Glazed salmon
Day 3	Smoked salmon and goat cheese scramble	Pan-broiled steak	One apple	Sour cream and Cuke salad
Day 4	Backward pizza	Pepperoncini spinach	One orange	Pork with a camembert sauce
Day 5	Rodeo eggs	Asparagus with curried walnut butter	Low-fat fruit yogurt	Pepperoncini beef
Day 6	Buffalo wing omelet	Sopa tlalpeñ	Two sticks of celery filled with One and ¾ ounces of low-fat sof	Asparagus with curried walnut butter
Day 7	Perfect protein pancakes	Chicken in creamy orange sauce	Reduced-fat whole grain cookie	Chicken-chili-cheese salad

Week 19

	Breakfast	Lunch	Snack	Dinner
Day 1	Monterey scramble	Chicken breasts stuffed with artichokes and garlic cheese	One and a half ounces of dried apricots	Rib-eye steak with wine sauce
Day 2	Club omelet	Glazed salmon	Reduced-fat whole grain cookie	Easy Italian beef
Day 3	Fried mush	Roasted curried cauliflower	Reduced-fat whole grain cookie	Lemon-herb chicken breast
Day 4	Confetti frittata	Avocado and brown rice sala	Low-fat fruit yogurt	Pesto shrimp
Day 5	Parmesan-rosemary eggs	Japanese fried rice	One banana	Cumin mushrooms
Day 6	Coconut flax bread	Dragon's tee	Low-fat fruit yogurt	Roman lamb steak
Day 7	Smoked salmon and goat cheese scramble	Cranberry-peach turkey roast	Reduced-fat whole grain cookie	Sautéed mushrooms and spinach with pepperon

Week 20

	Breakfast	Lunch	Snack	Dinner
Day 1	Insta-quiche	Not-quite-middle-eastern salad	Two sticks of celery filled with One and ¾ ounces of low-fat sof	Toasted salad
Day 2	Buffalo wing omelet	Not-quite-middle-eastern salad	One low-fat/low-sugar cereal bar	Bleu burger
Day 3	Confetti frittata	Two-cheese cauliflower	Reduced-fat whole grain cookie	Chicken-almond rice
Day 4	Smoked salmon and goat cheese scramble	Gingered monkfish	Reduced-fat whole grain cookie	Sun-dried tomato-portobello salmon roast
Day 5	Insta-quiche	Pan-broiled steak	Reduced-fat whole grain cookie	Maple-spice country-style ribs
Day 6	Backward pizza	Roman lamb steak	One and a half ounces of dried apricots	Spinach-plum salad
Day 7	Monterey jack and avocado omelet	Mushroom risotto	Seven ounces of skim milk	Sour cream and Cuke salad

Week 21

	Breakfast	Lunch	Snack	Dinner
Day 1	Unpotato tortilla	Pork loin with red wine and walnuts	One low-fat/low-sugar cereal bar	Chicken-pecan salad
Day 2	Parmesan-rosemary eggs	Golden triangle chicken kabobs	One banana	Not-quite-middle-eastern salad
Day 3	Coconut flax bread	Gorgonzola-and-pesto Caesar salad	Two sticks of celery filled with One and ¾ ounces of low-fat sof	Old Fashioned Salmon Soup
Day 4	Confetti frittata	Sun-dried tomato-portobello salmon roast	One apple	Chili-bacon scallops
Day 5	California omelet	Baked clams	Low-fat fruit yogurt	Not-quite-middle-eastern salad
Day 6	Pork rind waffles	Pork loin with red wine and walnuts	One pear	Meatza
Day 7	Salted caramel–cinnamon pancak	Bleu burger	One banana	Roman lamb steak

Conclusion

Thank you for making it to the end of this book. I trust that you have learned a lot about nutrition and diet for diabetes. The ball is now in your court concerning taking care of your health. Remember, diabetes is not a life sentence, and it can be managed to the point where you enjoy all aspects of your life.

You must take care of yourself by going natural when it comes to the food you eat and including at least 30 minutes of physical exercise every day.

Spread the word to your friends and family, and let us help spread awareness about diabetes, which we need to manage and treat.

Good health is the best gift you can give yourself! All the best!

Measurement conversion chart

Here are some conversion tables to help you measure recipes accurately.

CUPS	TBSP	TSP	ML
1	16	48	250
3/4	12	36	175
2/3	11	32	150
1/2	18	24	125
1/3	5	16	70
1/4	4	12	60
1/8	2	6	30
1/16	1	3	15

Cooking Conversion Chart

Measurement

CUP	ONCES	MILLIMETERS	TABLESPOONS
8 cup	64 oz	1895 ml	128
6 cup	48 oz	1420 ml	96
5 cup	40 oz	1180 ml	80
4 cup	32 oz	960 ml	64
2 cup	16 oz	480 ml	32
1 cup	8 oz	240 ml	16
3/4 cup	6 oz	177 ml	12
2/3 cup	5 oz	158 ml	11
1/2 cup	4 oz	118 ml	8
3/8 cup	3 oz	90 ml	6
1/3 cup	2.5 oz	79 ml	5.5
1/4 cup	2 oz	59 ml	4
1/8 cup	1 oz	30 ml	3
1/16 cup	1/2 oz	15 ml	1

Temperature

FAHRENHEIT	CELSIUS
100 °F	37 °C
150 °F	65 °C
200 °F	93 °C
250 °F	121 °C
300 °F	150 °C
325 °F	160 °C
350 °F	180 °C
375 °F	190 °C
400 °F	200 °C
425 °F	220 °C
450 °F	230 °C
500 °F	260 °C
525 °F	274 °C
550 °F	288 °C

Weight

IMPERIAL	METRIC
1/2 oz	15 g
1 oz	29 g
2 oz	57 g
3 oz	85 g
4 oz	113 g
5 oz	141 g
6 oz	170 g
8 oz	227 g
10 oz	283 g
12 oz	340 g
13 oz	369 g
14 oz	397 g
15 oz	425 g
1 lb	453 g

Beaking Measurement

If a recipe calls for this amount	You can also measure it this way
Dash	2 or 3 drops (liquid) or less than 1/8 teaspoon of (dry)
One tablespoon of	Three teaspoons or Half ounce
Two tablespoons of	1 ounce
A quarter cup of	Four tablespoons or 2 ounces
1/3 cup	Five tablespoons plus one teaspoon
Half cup of	Eight tablespoons or 4 ounces
3/4 cup	12 tablespoons of or 6 ounces
One cup of	16 tablespoons or 8 ounces
1 pint	2 cups or 16 ounces or 1 pound
1 quart	Four cups of or 2 pints
1 gallon	4 quarts
1 pound	16 ounces

Temperature Conversion

Fahrenheit	Celsius
32	0
212	100
250	120
275	140
300	150
325	160
350	180
375	190
400	200
425	220
450	230
475	240
500	260

Volume Measurement

US Units	Canadian Units	Australian Units
A quarter teaspoon of	1 ml	1 ml
Half teaspoon of	2 ml	2 ml
One teaspoon of	5 ml	5 ml
One tablespoon of	15 ml	20 ml
A quarter cup of	50 ml	60 ml
1/3 cup	75 ml	80 ml
Half cup of	125 ml	125 ml
2/3 cup	150 ml	170 ml
3/4 cup	175 ml	190 ml
One cup of	250 ml	250 ml
1 quart	1 liter	1 liter
One and a half quarts	One and a half liters	One and a half liters
2 quarts	2 liters	2 liters
Two and a half quarts	2.5 liters	2.5 liters
3 quarts	3 liters	3 liters
4 quarts	4 liters	4 liters

Weight Measurement

US Units	Canadian Units	Australian Units
1 ounce	30 grams	30 grams
2 ounces	55 grams	60 grams
3 ounces	85 grams	90 grams
4 ounces (1/4 pound)	115 grams	125 grams
8 ounces (half a pound)	225 grams	225 grams
16 ounces (1 pound)	455 grams	500 grams (half a kilogram)

Made in the USA
Coppell, TX
02 March 2023